Law and Order and School

*Daily Life in an Educational
Program for Juvenile Delinquents*

Law *and* Order *and* School

Daily Life in an Educational Program for Juvenile Delinquents

Shira Birnbaum

 Temple University Press
Philadelphia

Temple University Press, Philadelphia 19122
Copyright © 2001 by Temple University
All rights reserved
Published 2001
Printed in the United States of America

⊗ The paper used in this publication meets the requirements of the
American National Standard for Information Sciences–Permanence
of Paper for Printed Library Materials, ANSI Z39.48-1984

Library of Congress Cataloging-in-Publication Data

Birnbaum, Shira, 1962–
    Law and order and school : daily life in an educational program
for juvenile delinquents / Shira Birnbaum.
        p.   cm.
    Includes bibliographical references and index.
    ISBN 1-56639-869-X (cloth : alk. paper) – ISBN 1-56639-870-3
(pbk. : alk. paper)
        1. Juvenile delinquents–Education–United States–Case studies.
    2. Alternative schools–United States–Case studies.   I. Title.

HV9081 .B57 2001
371.93–dc21   00-051156

For Billy, Helen, and Dan

Contents

Acknowledgments

SUPPORT FROM MANY SOURCES enabled the completion of this book. Foremost were the students, teachers, and administrators at the school where the research was conducted. Peter Easton, Vandra Masemann, Manny Shargel, Isaac Eberstein, Daniel Maier-Katkin, David Palmer, and Kris Minor offered advice during the research and commented on drafts of the report. Employees at a variety of government agencies provided important data and documents. At Temple University Press, Doris Braendel and two reviewers offered guiding commentary about the manuscript. From Joy Moore and Sandra Martinez, I derived a sense of camaraderie on the parenting front, and Ruth, Dave, Rose, and Ralph supported our extended family as I finished my work. My husband Bill and my children Daniel and Helen shared their luminous beauty and unending wisdom.

1

Introduction

THE DRIVERS ARRIVE before sunrise; morning fog still drapes the school building and the creek alongside it. They are here for the vans. These are special vans, painted white like the ones used in this city to ferry prisoners. By 6:30 A.M., they are fanning out on their morning pick-up routes. One heads west from the school and then traces a southward arc around the city limits, stopping to collect children from the string of cluttered trailer parks that fringes the pine woods. Another heads downtown, cutting a jagged line through a district of ramshackle wooden houses, mostly rentals, and abandoned lots dense with wisteria and kudzu. Several encampments of homeless men and women are warming themselves around drums of burning trash; revitalization plans have been proposed for this area. The third van heads north, beyond the sprawling new suburbs, along the edges of fenced-in former cotton and tobacco fields now converted to private quail-hunting estates. A few children will be picked up from the smaller surrounding rural towns. One of the vans makes a quick stop at the city homeless shelter, where a fourteen-year-old boy is already waiting at the door. This is a booming Southern city. With a large number of federal and state government offices and two universities, unemployment is low; the suburbs are expanding rapidly northward. But here are the neighborhoods of the poor. Forty teenagers, mostly black males, some wearing electronic monitors strapped around their ankles, are still wiping the sleep from their eyes as their vans pull into the school parking lot around 8:30 A.M. Teachers are waiting to greet them at the gate; homeroom starts in about twenty minutes.

This book is a study of a private alternative school program for troubled teenagers in a midsize Southern city. Under contract jointly with the local public school district and the state juvenile justice agency, the school, referred to here by the pseudonym Academy,[1] enrolled between forty and fifty students, all repeat lawbreakers expelled or temporarily removed from their public schools either by juvenile courts, public school officials, or state agency caseworkers. This study focuses on the organization and culture of the school, on issues of curriculum, pedagogy, behavior management, and classroom environment, the mundane features of everyday internal life that frame students' experiences and, ultimately, program outcomes. The aim was to grasp the forms of social and cultural knowledge and self-understanding being fostered among the students and to see what processes inside and outside the building were helping or hindering the attainment of the educational and rehabilitative goals set forth by official policy.

Alternative Education Programs as Subjects for Research

Several factors have combined to enable a recent expansion and proliferation around the United States of a variety of alternative educational programs, like Academy, affiliated with or managed jointly by a combination of educational, juvenile justice, and social service agencies. First, teacher union leaders and parent groups in the late 1980s gave voice to a growing sentiment that violent or difficult-to-manage students should be removed from regular classrooms. Before his death in 1997, Albert Shanker, longtime president of the American Federation of Teachers, called upon school districts to establish alternative placements for these students (Hill 1998). Despite fears about the cost of such programs and long-standing concerns about the potential for educational inequality that might result from segregation of the most challenging children (Lawrence, Steed, and Young 1984; Coulby and Harper 1985), school administrators responded aggressively, seeking placements that might be more successful for the students and would not lead to politically damaging increases in reportable dropout rates (Young 1990).[2] A host of private entrepreneurs entered the picture as subcontractors, offering a menu of program options and features. During the 1990s, legislation was introduced in more than half of all states, including Arkansas, California, Colorado, Florida, Georgia, Hawaii, Illinois, Indiana, Louisiana, Maryland, Minnesota, Mississippi, Missouri, Nebraska, Nevada, New Hampshire, New Jersey, North Dakota, Ohio, Oklahoma, Oregon, Pennsylvania, South Carolina, South Dakota, Tennessee, Texas, Utah, Virginia, Washington, West Virginia, Wisconsin, and Wyoming, to enable or regulate the provision of alternative educational services to violent or disruptive students (National Conference of State Legislatures 1999a). A few states, including Arizona and Kansas, had had such legislation on the books already.

Meanwhile, a series of civil rights lawsuits and the subsequent administrative restructuring of juvenile justice systems in many states in the 1980s and early 1990s (Feld 1993) was leading to the replacement of a long-standing but trouble-plagued "reform school" system with a network of smaller-scale community-based programs and services for troubled children (Lerman 1984; Miller 1998). Private entrepreneurs in those years became a large and growing proportion of the providers of such programs (Leone, Rutherford, and Nelson 1991; Bakal and Lowell 1992; United States Department of Justice 1988). Federal laws passed in the 1970s and 1980s guaranteeing the provision of educational services to handicapped children, regardless of legal or custody status,[3] moreover, meant that new juvenile justice programs would require some formal educational focus or component (Coffey and Gemignani 1994; Leone 1990); many delinquency services formerly classified as "treatment" or "rehabilitation" now had to be framed as specifically "educational" as well, and could become subject, in at least some cases, to explicit management, accreditation, or regulatory scrutiny by state or local education agencies (Leone, Price, and Vitolo 1986). Lawsuits regarding the availability and adequacy of educational services in juvenile justice settings began to multiply (Robinson and Rapport 1999; Warboys and Schauffer 1986). In the wake of studies suggesting that few juvenile justice programs were actually in a position to comply with the new laws, the federal government in the 1990s introduced policy initiatives calling for increased coordination among federal, state, and local agencies as well as private subcontractors providing educational services to delinquent children (National Association of State Directors of Special Education 1998; Ingersoll and LeBoeuf 1997; Hellriegel and Yates 1999; Robinson and

Rapport 1999; Tapper, Kleinman, and Nakashian 1997; Gemignani 1994). Between 1994 and 1998, in response to the growth and diversity of community programs and facilities and questions regarding oversight responsibility, legislatures in eighteen states introduced measures regulating the provision of educational services to delinquent youths in state custody, in some cases specifically requiring coordinated efforts by juvenile justice and educational authorities (National Conference of State Legislatures 1999b).

What has resulted from a decade of developments in this area is a complex patchwork of thousands of local juvenile justice programs that offer educational services through a variety of joint institutional and agency affiliations.[4] Increasingly, such programs are small and privately managed; the public generally has little access to what goes on inside them and little knowledge regarding how—or in fact whether—they achieve any of their stated goals (Coffey and Gemignani 1994; Leone, Rutherford, and Nelson 1991).

Our culture emphasizes contrasts between childhood and adulthood. The adult has a job, a car, a vote, and in some cases a gun. The child is unemployed and propertyless; he or she has few public, legal, or political obligations. The adult strives to be a leader and to assert dominance over others or at least equality with them. The child must display deference or submission to elders and even strangers. Adults drink, smoke, and engage in sexual activities and parenthood. To these the child is exhorted to "just say no." Noncompliance becomes grounds for punishment. At the border of these discontinuities is adolescence. Even for children born to families with wealth and social success, adolescence can be fraught with personal trials. It is all the more so for those who enter life in poverty or family instability or both, and especially so for those who break the law, drop out or are removed from public school, or enter the often maze-like network of state social service and criminal justice agencies. For society as a whole and for the children and adolescents themselves, much depends on what can be accomplished by the educational, social, and civic institutions charged with guiding the transition to adult life. As new institutional forms emerge, it becomes increasingly important to investigate their character and the qualitative effects they might have on the people who come into contact with them. Whatever is promised in the name of such institutions, whether by educators, judges, agency caseworkers or legislators, it is in fact only the day-to-day lived reality of these places that ultimately fixes their meaning for those on the inside.

Each generation, in education and in criminal justice as in other areas of civic and political life, works to some degree from the assumptions, institutional and political structures, and linguistic and ideological conventions it inherits from the past. Academy's structure and official techniques drew from formal procedural rules as well as professional conventions given by the public bureaucracies charged with managing and regulating the program. At the school's core, however, were the struggles of teachers—most of them very young and new to the work, many of them steeped in the unique evangelical religious traditions of Southern culture—to derive moral meaning, job satisfaction, and a sense of accomplishment from a demanding and frequently painful work setting. There were also the strivings of the young students—black and white, male and female, many of them living in extreme poverty and under conditions of almost breathtaking family strife—to become adults with the style, power, and grace to which teenagers everywhere aspire.

Cultural and organizational processes in schools are always related in some way, directly or indirectly, to processes and structures in the broader society, to the constellation of values, beliefs, and institutional dynamics in the world outside the school (Apple 1979; Apple and Weis 1983; Bourdieu and Passeron 1977; Bowles and Gintis 1976; Carnoy and Levin 1985; Everhart 1983a, 1983b; Weis 1988; Willis 1977). This study of one school building is, in this vein, a study of what can happen between students and teachers more generally in an intensely politically charged atmosphere and under conditions where long-term outcomes are highly uncertain. In the chapters that follow, it will be seen how students and teachers negotiated a path through the conditions that framed their encounters with one another.

The Setting

Academy opened its doors in 1993. The city and its surrounding countryside, like many urban areas in the South, had seen rapid growth in recent decades; population had nearly doubled by 1990 to almost 200,000, according to local planning commission statistics. More than 40 percent of city workers in 1995 were employed in federal, state, or local government offices, with another 25 percent in services, predominantly health care, and 19 percent in the retail sector. Median family household income, comparatively high for the South due to the prevalence of government employment, neared $37,000 in 1995. The city was home to 50,000 students, a community college, and two universities. One fifth of city residents were under age eighteen, another fifth age eighteen to twenty-four. Average annual unemployment hovered below 3 percent, considerably lower than in the rest of the nation, but the large population of students seeking part-time work created conditions of widespread underemployment. Housing and community development officials reported that many workers seeking full-time jobs, including, for instance, the teenagers at Academy and in many cases their troubled parents as well, were persistently unable to find them.

Several ambitious public projects had been launched in recent years in tandem with population growth, including construction of a major research and business office park complex, a new jail, and a public sports arena. The city was experiencing a housing boom reflecting its bifurcated wage structure. About 40 percent of housing units added after 1980 were single-family homes, mostly aimed at middle-class homebuyers settling predominantly in the northeastern sections. Another 20 percent, according to planning commission reports, were mobile homes catering to lower-income residents; these were located for the most part in the city's south side. The surrounding rural countryside was marked by high unemployment and long-standing poverty typical of the region as a whole, with much of the work involving seasonal employment in farming, fishing, or logging industries or temporary work in a recent rural growth industry, prison construction. City and county planners and political leaders occupied themselves with the issues of road improvement, housing construction, school crowding, and solid waste management that accompany rapid urban growth.

The city was widely recognized as having been one of the centers of the civil rights movement of the 1950s and 1960s; activists had staged sit-ins at whites-only lunch counters, and local church leaders had gone on to take key positions in national civil rights organizations. Cross burnings by the Ku Klux Klan had made national news headlines, as had vigorous attempts by local white citizen groups to maintain segregated swimming pools, bus stations, and movie theaters. But racial divisions continued to be the norm well into the 1990s. Police had recently scuffled with black residents of a public housing project, who claimed excessive force had been used against them. A white university employee on a drunken rampage killed a black teenager by intentionally ramming his truck at high speed into the back of the teen's car on one of the city's major traffic arteries, according to news reports. The region had made national and international news headlines in recent months when white administrators of a church in one of the nearby rural towns allegedly demanded the disinterment from the church cemetery of a deceased biracial infant; they later reneged and, in front of television cameras, apologized to the baby's parents.

Though in 1995 almost a third of the city's residents and a fourth of the county's residents were black, blacks had been elected to public office for the first time only in the 1990s, as in much of the South, after activists won rancorous court cases requiring the replacement of city- and county-wide voting arrangements with a system of smaller representative districts in school board and local government elections. Median annual family household income among blacks was only 53 percent that among whites; 30 percent of all black residents were living below the federal poverty level. In 1990, according to the U.S. Census, one in four black households had no car, and one in twelve had no phone.

Schools had been legally desegregated by court order in the early 1970s after decades of local white opposition to integration, but of the two dozen public elementary schools in the city, three older facilities in the highly racially segregated central city had student populations more than 95 percent black. A number of private schools had been built during the desegregation era to accommodate white flight from district schools; their enrollments continued to be nearly exclusively white. Enrollment was predominantly white in the newly opened public schools serving the expanding and mostly white suburban developments. Reports of apparent racial bias in school discipline had made headlines almost from the first days of integration. In 1973, a much-publicized statewide study revealed that large numbers of black students were being suspended from newly integrated schools in many towns. In the wake of national media attention, the state's school systems began to experiment with ways to circumvent suspension and expulsion, devising innovations such as special detention rooms or other out-of-classroom programs, antecedents in some ways to some varieties of contemporary alternative school.

Overall student achievement in local schools was low. In the 1994–95 school year, according to district figures, the graduation rate was less than 73 percent; school retention rates averaged 15 percent. At one district high school with a predominantly black student population, a fourth of the students had been held back. Among the several hundred local high school graduates who had enrolled in community colleges or universities in the state, fewer than 60 percent had passed a state-administered postsecondary readiness exam, according to district statistical reports. The state as a whole ranked among the lowest in the nation not only in terms of student achievement but also in terms of per-pupil educational spending.

The region was politically and socially conservative, mirroring much of the rest of the South, with church attendance high and the dominant religious affiliation Baptist and evangelical. Most summer weekends it was possible to find a tent revival in some part of town. Long dominated in the political arena by conservative Southern Democrats and more recently by New South Republicans, both the city and the county had turned somewhat rightward in recent years. Elections had brought to local government several self-proclaimed Christian fundamentalists, including a creationist who had joined the school board. Voters elected law enforcement and court personnel who advocated an end to the "coddling" of criminals, state legislators had recently talked of reinstating the "chain gang" for state prisoners, and administrators in the local sheriff's office were implementing a plan by which jail inmates would be required to work for their food.

A legislative restructuring of school discipline was under way in the state, with important consequences for private entrepreneurs in juvenile justice and in education. A "safe schools" law had passed in the mid-1990s with the support of a broad coalition of teachers, parents, and political leaders. It facilitated the legal removal of disruptive children from public school classrooms, waiving key school-system rules in order to enable the establishment of alternative educational programs–"last chance schools," as they came to be called–to which the students could be assigned. There was evidence, however, of racial bias in public school discipline and, as a logical consequence, in the patterns by which students might potentially be ousted to alternative placements. An investigation sponsored jointly by the state education and juvenile justice agencies found that one out of every five black high school students in the local school district and more than one out of every four black middle school students had been suspended out of school at some point during the year, compared with 12 percent of white high school and middle school students. Investigators noted that in the state overall, for the same offenses, black students seemed more likely than whites to receive harsh disciplinary action and ultimately to be expelled from school entirely.

In 1992, a group of regional business and civic leaders convened a juvenile crime study team. Statistics indicated a problem: with a more than 240 percent increase in juvenile felony arrests between 1983 and 1993, the county had experienced one of the nation's largest increases in juvenile crime, particularly felony crime. The biggest increases, moreover, were among juveniles thirteen to fourteen years old. Rates of arrest for car theft, burglary, concealed firearms, and cocaine possession had skyrocketed so that by 1992 the rate of arrest among juveniles was higher than in practically any other county in the state. On the street, getting arrested had become practically a rite of passage among some segments of the population. Team investigators noted that there were limited sentencing and local programmatic alternatives for lawbreaking children: the county had relatively few rehabilitation programs or halfway houses. They called upon state and local government officials, as well as private investors, to expand the options.

The Political Context

The state's juvenile justice system was in the midst of a major reorganization. Plagued historically by low standards of accountability and a track record of violence and brutality against young lawbreakers, the system had promised justice but for many years delivered something considerably less. Some years earlier, a federal class action suit had been filed on behalf of a young teenager confined in one of the state-run reform schools for delinquent children. Alleging severely overcrowded conditions, beatings by supervisors, denials of food, overuse of solitary confinement, and inadequate medical and educational services, the suit named as defendants the governor, the head of the state social services agency, the education commissioner, and the reform school superintendent. The state had not complied with a 1974 federal law requiring the separation of violent criminals from petty offenders, with the result that rapists were being held alongside school truants in very crowded conditions. Students were subjected to continuous threats of physical as well as psychological harm, and disproportionate numbers of them were black. To the students and their families, the criteria for getting released from the reform schools seemed as inconsistent and elusive as the criteria for getting in.

After years of wrangling, the parties had entered into a consent decree approved by the federal court.[5] The plan was to reduce the number of children housed in the reform schools, provide formal procedures for admission and release, and establish educational and health programs in line with the children's needs. A court monitor was appointed to report on compliance. Overnight, hundreds of children were transferred out of the reform schools as the state began efforts to comply with the federal court. The children quickly filled to capacity the existing limited array of smaller community-based drug or rehabilitation programs; those in the "overflow" were either released to the community, where some committed new crimes, or were placed in detention facilities to await new court processing or program assignments. Studies by watchdog organizations soon revealed a host of new legal violations. Delays in case processing resulted subsequently in detention lasting far longer, for many children, than what state civil rights laws formally allowed. Once again, facility overcrowding was accompanied by reports of physical violence by supervisors against the children in their charge.[6]

State legislators responded to the crisis by passing a law that, on paper at least, promised to modernize the juvenile justice system in line with reforms that had been implemented elsewhere in the country. The law required the state social service agency to develop additional small-scale, community-based programs for the many nonviolent petty offenders who were still awaiting institutional placement. It called for the development of a formal instrument to assess young lawbreakers' educational and social service needs, and it mandated that medical and educational services be made available, as federal laws already required, in all rehabilitation programs and detention facilities. It called on judges to assign children to programs near their homes so as to facilitate their integration into the community after their release.

But legislative appropriations were slow in coming. Actual payments to the state's embattled social service agency were about half of what was originally promised, and once ambitious plans for program development and new facility construction were scaled back. Soon the list of children awaiting placement in rehabilitation programs had jumped again to 1,000 names; children were spending months locked in overcrowded detention facilities. Pressured to cut short the state waiting list, administrators at existing treatment programs started releasing juveniles after very short lengths of stay. Police departments, in turn, stepped up surveillance on the streets. Juvenile arrest rates went up, perhaps not surprisingly. In a political milieu where juvenile crime was now dominating daily news headlines, state attorneys began bypassing the juvenile courts entirely and transferring young lawbreakers into the adult criminal system. The situation amounted to precisely the opposite of what had been intended by federal juvenile justice reform legislation of the preceding two decades. The state corrections agency had recently embarked on a spree of prison-building; attorneys were making use of the available resources.

By the mid-1990s, a new crop of conservative legislators had been elected to public office throughout the state, including a coalition of religious fundamentalists, representing both political parties, who vowed to "get tough" on youth crime. Soon, with promises about injecting "moral principles" into political affairs, the legislature passed a massive, controversial bill signaling an unprecedented ideological break from what had been a twenty-year-long national trend toward rehabilitation-oriented programming for delinquent children. With tough-sounding language and new, harsher penalties for young lawbreakers, the law promised "sure punishment" of child offenders. It revised prevailing court sentencing structures, lowering the age at which children could be sent to adult criminal court and tried and sentenced as adults. It provided for the expansion of military-style "boot camps" for what criminologists call the "shock incarceration" of young repeat lawbreakers. For critics who complained that young people sent to adult court were receiving a youth "discount" (that is, sentences lighter or shorter than those given older lawbreakers), it also added a jail option—up to three years in an adult-style lock-up—as a new high-end penalty that could guarantee jail time for the most violent juvenile offenders even while segregating them, as federal law required, from adult criminals. The law increased the amount of time a child

could be held legally in a detention center awaiting placement and enabled a no-time-limit detention of children considered "high risks" to the community. It restored judges'
ability under certain circumstances to place status offenders–runaways and school truants–in detention centers alongside more violent offenders.

For all its harshness, however, the new law also offered
legal and social reforms that hinted at increasing procedural
rationality and, it was hoped, protecting children from some
of the inconsistencies that had characterized sentencing and
delinquency programming in the past. It established a com-
puterized state-wide network of assessment centers where
newly arrested children would undergo standardized bat-
teries of psychological and physical tests as an ostensibly
uniform basis for subsequent treatment and processing. It
also mandated the development of a formal instrument by
which delinquency treatment programs could be monitored
and evaluated. It provided that formal educational services
be delivered and monitored regularly in every delinquency
program, with coordination among a variety of state and
local educational and justice agencies, and it created a commission to design means for improving the training of youth
workers. The law called for cost-effectiveness studies and
set up an advisory board to collect statistics and evaluate
annually the bottom-line outcomes of what were by now an
increasing number of small-scale programs, many of them
privately run, serving delinquent youths.

Old problems persisted, however, at least in the beginning. Almost from opening day, reports started emerging of
physical violence against juveniles being held at the state's
newly created boot camps. Guards were suspended from at
least one such facility for what supervisors termed "exces-

sive use of force." Assaults against juveniles were reported
at one of the new jail-like facilities for repeat offenders. State
investigators noted staff underqualification and high
turnover rates at a variety of programs, and high-level
administrators at a detention center were fired when investigators charged that older children had been pressed into
service as a kind of surrogate police force to discipline the
younger inmates; according to newspaper reports, children
told of having their heads shoved into toilets and their bodies whipped with damp towels. Hundreds of children, meanwhile, continued to languish on the waiting list for placement, and juvenile detention centers were still severely
overcrowded, a few centers nearing 200 percent capacity at
some points during the year, according to state reports, placing acute supervisory burdens on program staff aware from
experience and from national surveys that twenty-five per
thousand juveniles held in detention will physically mutilate
themselves or threaten or attempt suicide (United States
Department of Justice Office of Juvenile Justice and Delinquency Prevention 1995a).

Delays in court processing of juvenile cases continued to
be a state norm, worse in some judicial districts than in others, and surveys by a state oversight board pointed to what
criminologists call a "justice by geography" wherein similar cases were being handled differently, and with varying
degrees of delay, across judicial regions and counties, with
children in some areas experiencing apparently harsher
treatment than children in others. Widely publicized local
studies indicated possible race and gender inequities as well,
with older children and black children in some regions tending to receive apparently harsher sentences than younger
children and whites, and girls receiving somewhat harsher

treatment in at least some cases than did boys with similar records.[7]

Moreover, treatment-program placements continued evidently to be guided as much by the whims and personal political orientations of judges and state attorneys as by any consistent formal policy standards or good-practices rule.[8] A searing state audit in 1995 indicated that more than half of all the children enrolled in one very large juvenile justice program had been legally eligible for a far less intensive regimen than had actually been prescribed for them. Four of five judges surveyed in the report claimed no knowledge of the most recent program-placement criteria promulgated by state agency staff; instead, they had opted to get as tough as possible on the children they sentenced. There were few checks on such caprice: not wanting to jeopardize good working relationships with judges and state attorneys, according to the audit, the children's case managers had in most cases agreed to the tougher sentences even when they contradicted official policy. Similar inconsistencies were revealed in internal evaluations of a sister program: state investigators found that the program was bringing into the criminal justice system large numbers of children whose crimes were too minor to trigger eligibility for government intervention. More than three-quarters of enrollees did not even meet the program's own placement criteria.[9]

Deficiencies plagued attempts to institute new educational programming. Surveys in 1995 by teams from the state education and juvenile justice agencies revealed a pervasive shortage of qualified personnel running what were being called educational services in programs for delinquents; there were widespread shortages of materials and classroom space and a dearth of procedures for assessing children's educational needs and progress. In violation of federal law, special-education students, by some estimates 30 to 40 percent of the national juvenile justice population,[10] were among the most severely underserved, with program staff displaying little knowledge, according to the report, of local, state, or federal educational policy or of the children's legal rights, and no grasp of what might constitute special educational needs or appropriate instructional strategies.[11]

Yet in numerical terms and as a proportion of all crime, youth arrests and detentions continued to rise.

Academy

Academy was run by a private nonprofit firm based outside the city. Just under thirty people worked in the building, seven of them full-time teachers supervising between forty and fifty students at any given time. Oversight by school district officials was handled under the umbrella of the local dropout prevention administration, which ran, at the same time, two public four-year alternative high schools, one of them a "school of choice" for students who were generally academically successful (this school was popular and well regarded and had a waiting list of applicants) and the other a "last chance" or "discipline" school for children permanently expelled from mainstream classes. The principal of the local "last chance" school held supervisory responsibility for the educational program at Academy and for the accreditation of its curriculum. The district was also providing or supervising subcontracted educational services at the regional juvenile detention center, a drug rehabilitation program, a program for "at-risk" teenage girls, and a number of other private rehabilitation or treatment facilities in the area that, like Academy, were contracted by the state juvenile justice agency and catered to children in various forms of custody or caseworker supervision. In total, almost 900 teenagers in the district in the 1995–96 school year were enrolled in programs affiliated with and funded jointly by the district and the state juvenile justice agency. Academy was part of the continuum of local educational programming being provided by this combination of institutions under laws mandating multi-agency coordination of educational services.

Roughly a third of the students at Academy had been legally "committed" for rehabilitation and treatment directly by the courts or by juvenile justice caseworkers, mostly for felony crimes such as burglary, car theft, or illegal weapons possession. All were what the state termed "low-risk youths"–people age fourteen to eighteen who posed no apparent immediate threat of violence to themselves or others. Another third, roughly, were public school students who had been on some type of probation, primarily for drug possession, but who subsequently had violated or threatened to violate probation rules, in most cases by skipping school repeatedly or failing to meet state-imposed bedtime curfews. The final third of Academy students had been assigned to the school as a transitional "step down," as caseworkers referred to it, from a reform school or residential rehabilitation or treatment program for violent or repeat lawbreakers. The local "last-chance" high school occasionally bumped over a particularly unruly probationer or two on a temporary basis, for only a few days or weeks. School staff referred to this small overflow population as "coming in for a tune-up."

The program at Academy was designed, ideally, to last six months, during which students were to take five classes a day and earn high school credit in preparation for a job or as a transition back to a longer-term school setting, or both. Academy was not required to pay the union-negotiated salaries earned by public school teachers or to hire school district custodians or bus drivers. It was designed to look and feel, however, like an ordinary, if short-term, version of public school: staff referred to themselves as teachers; there were five class periods, each lasting an hour; hot lunches in plastic foam containers were delivered every day from one of the local public school cafeterias; students were bused home in the afternoon; the successful students participated in a graduation ceremony involving cake, speeches, and caps and gowns. The curriculum included daily classes in English, math, history, and physical education; courses were offered as well in woodworking, oceanography, or marine science. Each class was matched to a course reference number on the school district's master list so that students could earn formal high school credit. Most of the Academy staff were not state-certified teachers, but the local superintendent had approved a rule exemption allowing three of them to make preliminary applications for teaching licenses and enroll in a district-sponsored teacher-orientation program.

There was a distinct absence of what delinquency workers call "hardware"–the locks and bars of the old-fashioned juvenile reform school. There were no secure fences, no razor wire. The intent, as a school promotional brochure characterized it, was to create an atmosphere of "raw, unadulterated affection" between students and staff. Special school events included periodic camping or fishing trips and an annual Olympics-style sports competition. In 1995 and 1996, Academy was rated by a team of state inspectors representing both juvenile justice and education agencies as one of the state's top programs for juvenile delinquents–out of several hundred–in its "delivery of educational services." Inspectors noted that students were taking courses approved by the state education department, that formal academic assessment forms had been filed by administrators, and that graduates had earned regular high school credits approved by the local public school board and potentially transferable in a transition back to public school.

Research Methods

Data for this study were obtained over a period of a year, during which visits were made to the school as well as to a variety of related state and local agencies and institutions. The primary method of research inside the school was participant observation. For part of the year and also before the research began, I worked as a basic skills tutor and classroom aide, spending between ten and forty hours per week in the building. I also chaperoned field trips and on occasion provided more general staff support, for example, by cleaning the oven or wiping down cabinets in the school kitchen, arranging chairs in the assembly hall in preparation for a ceremony, or photocopying papers for the teachers. At one point I "published," on my home computer, a single-issue school magazine compiled from writing and artwork I had assigned to several classes of students. I also edited a draft of a grant proposal the education director was hoping to use to secure supplies for the woodworking shop (the grant was never submitted). Throughout my stay I participated in and observed classrooms, field trips, assemblies, and staff meetings and reviewed curriculum materials and policy documents.

My research was widely known, but it was not regarded as particularly unusual because the school was open to visitors at all times and there were virtually always some non-regular-staff aides or volunteers, mostly college or university graduate students, who were observing the program as part of an internship or term project. Class, race, and religion all marked me as an outsider to the school.[12] Perhaps because of my age (the age of many students' parents and probably most of their former public school teachers) and certainly in part because of the presence of other volunteers in the building, however, it was not difficult for me to assume the role and duties of a quasi-official staff person. I went out for occasional lunches and dinners with the staff. Every so often someone would ask my opinion about a personal educational matter, such as when one of the staff was considering transferring his daughter out of her elementary school or when one of the teachers was thinking about applying to graduate school. In line with the terms of my research access to the school, I did not collect, review, or inquire about students' individual case history files, interview students or their family members, or discuss with any student his or her legal status or personal situation. My role as a tutor brought me particularly close to several students with whom I worked and conversed on a regular basis (and who eventually successfully graduated from the program), but it did not prevent me from observing general classroom events or interactions involving others in the building.

Popular conceptions of troubled teenagers explain school failure primarily in terms of the attributes of students themselves, as an outcome of personal or individual deficiencies or characteristics.[13] This study focuses instead on the ecology of the institution as a whole, on what has been called the "internal life" of a school as it evolves from the interplay of people, goals, organizational structure, history, and policy context.[14] Initially, I was guided in my observations by simple and basic questions: What is supposed to happen at the school? What actually happens? What do teachers do? How do the young people respond? How, in essence, does the school prepare adolescents for participation in the prevailing patterns of adult life in the community? I paid particular attention to school goals, purposes, and definitions; to teacher working conditions and the physical setting of the building; to staffing and training practices; to curriculum content, both formal and informal; to the articulation among related institutions upstream and downstream from the school; to instructional practices such as the organization of classroom space, the allocation of classroom time, patterns of teacher attention, methods of discipline, and the organization of academic work tasks; to student responses to instruction and discipline; to the means by which authority was established in classrooms and among staff members; to pressure from external sources within the community and the way the institution responded to them.

The strength of participant observation methodology, as opposed to social science research methods based on the testing of circumscribed hypotheses preselected by the researcher, is that ideally it enables the researcher to grasp, through direct experience, the point of view of the people inside the setting she is studying.[15] Sometimes this point of view is in line with the researcher's initial expectations about where the research will lead; sometimes it is in significant contrast. Juvenile justice loomed large in the community. My first awareness of the system stemmed from personal contacts: both of the teenage boys living on my block had served time in the local detention center; my own children's favorite babysitter had seen a brother enter, and then miserably fail, a boot camp; a teacher friend had had in her class a young boy whose trial and eventual conviction on murder charges had made major local headlines. The very ubiquitousness of juvenile justice, combined with the generally poor showing of local educational institutions, was what had struck me in the first place as something worth investigating. Yet the people with whom a researcher lives or works in close contact over long periods have, through their actions and their language, their concern with some issues and not others, their attention to some features of a situation and not others, an important role in shaping or directing the research. As I participated in and observed the daily life of the school, the staff and students there transformed my research of it. Watching them and hearing them, I came to regard my study not as an analysis of how some well-known troubles plaguing juvenile justice and education might be reflected at the level of one school, but rather as an exploration of the very complicated and sometimes tragically paradoxical ways in which students and teachers, each using the tools available to them, strive to make the most of a difficult situation, how they refuse to submit to its more brutal aspects, and how they protect themselves from humiliation and harm.

2

Students and Teachers

NOT EVERY TEACHER, and not necessarily even the so-called "best" teachers, can work successfully with students in juvenile justice settings. Educators and administrators in juvenile justice have tried, but there is no easy or consistent way to identify the distinct blend of traits and attitudes that makes some teachers a better match than others (Coffey and Gemignani 1994; Leone, Rutherford, and Nelson 1991). Academy teachers were indeed a group distinct from the average in education, as were their students. The school building, moreover, was somewhat unlike most ordinary schools.

Students

The students at Academy were, on average, just under sixteen years old and had had somewhere near two years of contact with the juvenile justice system. About two-thirds were black, and between a fourth and a fifth were girls, several of them mothers. In its demographic composition, Academy was similar to other privately run juvenile justice programs serving what the state termed "low-risk" youth.[1] Two girls became pregnant during the study, one, it was claimed, by an Academy classmate. Two of the boys became fathers. One student tested positive during the year for hepatitis B, another for tuberculosis. At least four had parents or siblings in prison; a boy who had been court-ordered to tour the county jail asked, during an Academy field trip there, to visit his big brother's cell pod (the staff declined). Two boys had parents who went into hiding during the year while fleeing from police drug raids, leaving empty cabinets and unpaid house bills. More than 85 percent of the young people at Academy were enrolled in the local school district's federal free or reduced lunch program. About half lived with only one parent or grandparent. Several had to move temporarily to the city homeless shelter at various times during the year as families were evicted from rental units or when domestic feuds escalated to the point of jeopardizing their safety. Most of the students came from one of the three neighborhoods in the city where poverty and crime were concentrated. A few lived in homes with no telephone service.

School policy was to admit only juveniles age fourteen through eighteen with no recent history of physical violence, arson charges, or ongoing medical problems. Exceptions had been made, however, in part because the school's director insisted that Academy should be what he called "an institutional good citizen" willing to help juvenile justice caseworkers with their hardest-to-place youths–those who because of age, medical condition, housing situation, or severity of legal charges did not meet the criteria for admission to other programs.[2] Suspending the usual criteria, he had agreed to admit a thirteen-year-old boy with a history of arson charges, a girl taking psychotropic medications who was awaiting placement in another facility that at the time was filled to capacity, and a boy with a history of violence who was being held temporarily until a space could be found for him in a "higher-level" treatment facility.

Skills tests placed Academy students on average at the seventh grade level in math and reading–two to five years behind chronological grade level and barely at the point of functional literacy and numeracy. However, the skills range was extremely wide, a situation that rendered it difficult to design an effective instructional strategy for the group.[3] Nine of fifty-six students whose scores were available in the fall of 1995 ranked at the twelfth grade level in reading, and one girl had come from the local school district's "gifted and talented" rolls.[4] But eight students ranked at the level of second graders or lower. In math, while six students ranked at the twelfth grade level, five ranked as third graders or lower.

The majority of the students had not attended public school regularly for at least several months and in some cases several years, as virtually all, regardless of their skill levels, had a history of truancy, tardiness, suspension, classroom failure, or some combination of these. One girl old enough to be a high school junior, for example, told staff that she had stopped attending school at the end of her first year and spent much of what would have been her second year in a drug rehabilitation center. An eighteen-year-old boy reported when he arrived at Academy that he hadn't set foot in a school building for nearly two years. Several of the students had already been expelled to the local "last chance" school before their assignment to Academy.

At one point during the year, nineteen students–nearly half–were on the local public school district's Special Education rolls. Their Individual Education Plans (IEPs), required by federal law, were filled out by the history teacher, who had inherited them from the public schools in a state of what he reported to be severe disarray. Law requires that these plans be updated at least annually; in the case of at least three students, however, there had been no updates for two years, it was reported in a staff meeting, and one student had evidently spent five years in the public schools with no review of her charts. Law also requires that parents as well as school administrators attend the meetings at which these plans are prepared; the history teacher complained bitterly that parents virtually never attended the meetings he scheduled.[5]

At the same time, students were well aware of their low standing in the public schools; most were able to relate, with varying degrees of accuracy, the name or at least the acronym of learning handicaps with which they had been labeled—"S.L.D," "A.D.D.," "E.H.," "L.D."—and a few boasted occasionally of "having files this thick" with disciplinary citations. Two students were enrolled in a "special diploma" track in public high school, a somewhat controversial "alternative" degree track for students deemed unable, generally for reasons of mental retardation, ever to qualify for a standard diploma.[6]

Some of the students were visibly disfigured. One boy's back and shoulders were covered with thick raised scars, the result, staff said, of an early-childhood encounter with a space-heater fire. A girl had hatch-marks extending from the edge of one eye back in a thin stripe toward the hairline—the remains of a knife wound. Many of the students revealed missing teeth, missing fingernails, and bald spots where hair had been scalded off. A boy arrived at school one day with much of his body covered in deep black and blue bruises, one in the center of his back in the shape of a sneaker, with tread marks clearly discernible. He had robbed a store, according to teacher discussions in the conference room; its owners had found him and applied their own personal discipline. Another boy started school with hard purple scabs over his forehead and nose. A girl came to school with her face severely bruised and scratched; a counselor contacted the state domestic abuse hotline.[7] Virtually all the girls sucked their thumbs; when at times a classroom grew hot or an assembly dragged on, they lay their heads down on tables, twisting their earlobes the way a baby does as it comforts itself into slumber. One pregnant girl suffered the usual physical exhaustion that accompanies late pregnancy; she spent a good deal of class time sleeping with her head on a desk and her thumb, with its long nail polished a deep crimson, propped between open lips.

Most students arrived at Academy with a good deal of very obvious bitterness toward adults in positions of authority over them. Stories of having been "fucked" by judges, educators, or caseworkers were among the most common topics of animated conversation among the students. With school attendance a condition of probation, skipping public school classes had constituted for some of them an actual legal violation that was punishable by assignment to Academy. One boy had been picked up by police for carrying marijuana seeds in his pocket and had been placed on probation, a relatively straightforward arrangement requiring him periodically to report to a caseworker. But after a truancy officer caught him skipping classes at the local high school one day, his original sentence was escalated to include removal from public school and enrollment in the more regimented Academy program. He would tell this story heatedly to virtually anyone who entered the building, his classmates adding variations from their own experience. The sense of being "stuck" in a web where relatively minor infractions could become easily magnified into escalating legal charges was a source of tremendous and very public resentment for the students, who frequently could be overhead discussing among themselves the "fucked up" nature of "how they get you" and how "they think they own you." In this way, even as they were not a subject of daily conversation among teachers, many of whom rarely read the case files, students' private legal histories formed a prominent part of the daily discourse in and about the school.[8]

Students also brought to school an array of racial, cultural, and gender stereotypes and hostilities reflective of attitudes present to one degree or another in the community at large, posing, not surprisingly, another layer of challenges for the staff.[9] White students at various times during the study proclaimed their hatred, for instance, of "niggers," "nigga-monkeys," and "cheese-doodle-heads." Black students announced similar feelings for "rednecks," "faggot country boys," "blue-eyed devil bitches," "crackers," and "militiamen." The parents, too, sometimes displayed racial hostilities, several of them being known to slam doors in the faces of visiting Academy teachers of a race not their own. On the other hand, there was also some inter-racial dating; two of the white girls in the school had dated two of the black boys in their classes. Sexual themes were commonplace in conversation and daily interaction in the school. Instances in which boys put their hands on girls' buttocks in the lunchroom or while passing between classes were recorded on an almost daily basis, as were instances of girls being called "whore," "bitch," or "pussy." For some of the girls, sex was an important feature of public identity. One girl whose name started with the letter K took to the habit of signing her school papers with the phrase "Special K, Sexual Chocolate," in reference, apparently, to a breakfast cereal. Another girl repeatedly announced in class that she was "coming" because a particular boy had chosen to sit next to her.

Staff

Seven full-time teachers worked at Academy, along with eighteen or nineteen other full- or part-time employees (the number varied somewhat during the course of the year) who drove the school vans, ran the office, or provided state- or school district–mandated counseling, outreach, or supervisory services. With a few exceptions, school employees were under age thirty-five, a handful still in college. Of the seven teachers, five were in their twenties; one was in his early thirties. Black staff were the majority, and four of the teachers were black. The white employees were the school's executive director, the education director, the secretary, the building receptionist, and three teachers. Almost everyone on staff had been born in the region or had lived there for many years, and two of the community liaisons were ordained Baptist ministers. The school was demographically significantly unlike most ordinary public schools in the nation, where there is a pervasive shortage of minority teachers.[10] In fact, Academy was regarded by all the staff as a place where black and white employees could work side by side, where staff and students could forge strong personal bonds based on certain shared local experiences, and where blacks could move up the ranks. The director promoted one particularly well-liked black teacher to a management position within less than a year of her arrival.

Marcus, the math teacher, and Sherry, who taught physical education, had both recently graduated from a historically black college in the region, where they studied criminal justice. Soft-spoken and mild-mannered despite having the massive physique of a former college football player, Marcus intended eventually to become a social-work counselor and mentor to inner-city children. He and his wife had a newborn at home; the baby was colicky, demands at home were high, and Marcus found himself torn between work and home obligations. Sherry, at twenty-two the youngest staff member, was similarly easygoing and idealistic; her friendly relations with staff and students alike made her most popular among the other teachers. Having played basketball in college, she considered herself an activist on behalf of women's athletics and was ever reminding the female students that lifting weights and building muscles were a means of gaining control over their bodies and, indirectly, their lives. Cindy, the English teacher, was a gregarious and outspoken black woman who held a master's degree in public administration. Deaconess of her Baptist church and active with her minister husband in religious outreach to city youth groups, she was known by students as "the church lady" because of a tendency to carry around a Bible and pepper everyday conversation with religious quotations and exhortations. Frequently referring to herself as "living in that grace, with the Lord," Cindy almost daily admonished students: "Be thankful that God let you see another day." Dwayne, who taught the boating class, was a black Puerto Rican with a college degree in art; he had spent much of his life sailing or repairing boats and had come to Academy because "It's the only job I know in this town where you can be on the water almost every day." He had a baby daughter at home; he and his wife lived within walking distance of the school.

Travis, the white vocational teacher, had graduated from one of the private Christian high schools that had been established to accommodate white flight during the desegregation era. A one-time handyman, he cultivated what students called a "redneck" appearance, usually wearing military fatigues, heavy workboots, and a military-style "buzz" haircut; he was also a self-taught guitarist active in the local music scene. Divorced, battling for custody of a young daughter, Travis lived alone in a trailer on a farm outside the city, where he did farmwork in lieu of paying rent, working an extra weekend job as a gas station mechanic. Rick, the history teacher and at forty-three the oldest staff member, was regarded with some suspicion by most of the other staff and with almost universal hostility by the students. He was the only teacher who openly opposed the school policy ban on corporal punishment, lamenting at one meeting that "a lickin' with a phone cord would do these kids a world of good." Rick had a degree from a Baptist Bible college and had held an assortment of previous jobs–traveling salesman, substitute school teacher, resident parent in a runaway shelter. The only Academy teacher who had had any traditional teacher training and previous classroom experience, he'd earned several credits toward a master's degree in education some years earlier and had spent more than a year working as a full-time substitute teacher in a public middle school in another city. Laura, who taught the marine science classes, had recently graduated college as a biology major. Although she was an expert scuba diver with considerable physical strength and extensive training in the martial arts, her long blond hair and pale white skin gave her a somewhat girlish appearance, which became a constant source of trouble for her at the school. Laura worried about an ailing mother who lived practically across the country and was undergoing cancer treatments.

Also on staff were three part-time bus drivers, two or three part-time monitors whose job was to phone students at home in the evening to track compliance with court-imposed curfews or to collect from the streets any students who were skipping class, three community liaisons who accompanied students to court appearances and helped them find job or school placements after finishing the program, a family outreach counselor (this position remained vacant for about half a year, however), and four counselors who supervised the third of Academy students transitioning from institutions for violent offenders. At the management level the school had a discipline supervisor (for part of the year, with the somewhat confusing title of "training coordinator") who monitored disruptive students removed from their classrooms, an executive director, an assistant director, an office manager, and an education director. Kevin, the education director, was the sole formally certified teacher on the school staff, and he frequently doubled as a classroom substitute when regular teachers were out. Kevin talked often about the "intrinsic rewards" of working at Academy, rewards he believed to be far greater than those available to teachers working with more traditional students. The school also had a building receptionist who doubled as an attendance monitor. A second assistant director had been on staff for a brief time; he was asked to leave after a scuffle with some of the students and was not replaced.

Almost from the day Academy opened, there had been problems with managerial staffing. The school's first executive director, a retired professional football player, had had little experience either in management or in education. The local public school district had charged Academy with reneging on its contract: records were in disarray; credentials of the teaching staff did not match those required by the district; classes had not been adequately matched to district-approved curricula, and students played basketball when the schedule called for English or math; Individual Education Plans (IEPs), required by federal law for handicapped students, had not been completed. When, after the first year, the school district threatened to cancel Academy's contract and withhold public school funds, Academy's parent firm installed a new director and sent an energetic educational supervisor to renegotiate the school district contract, rally the staff, and revise the curriculum in line with district criteria.

Sean, the new executive director, had been born and raised in the region and spent ten years working inside the juvenile justice system, where he was regarded universally as a talented "kids person" at ease even with the most difficult students. Zealously casual and plainspoken, with no college training, he had spent time in the military and competed for regional weightlifting titles. Sean wore blue jeans to work and chewed tobacco furiously in his office when students weren't watching. A hands-on manager, he was ever wandering the building, shaking hands with students, inquiring after family, schoolwork, and long-term plans, often joining students assigned to work crews for disciplinary infractions. Sean harbored a great deal of suspicion toward what he called "the guys with the polished fingernails" who occupied the halls of the state legislature and "talked out of both sides of their mouth." As a teenager, he had scuffled with police—an experience, he claimed, which "taught me that every kid deserves another chance." Sean was a born-again Christian; he kept a Bible on his office desk and insisted as a matter of school policy that "everybody can have his life turned around." This was a first principle, announced with fervor in school assemblies and repeated with great frequency among staff, whom Sean was continually exhorting: "Find the good—save that life." Staff admired Sean for the friendliness and dignified ease of his relations with students; they found his optimism, however, consistently annoying, even saccharine; a few considered it a sign that Sean had "lost touch" with matters of classroom management. Almost everyone, moreover, harbored some degree of bitterness, much of it directed toward Sean, about low wages, infrequent raises, and requests that they "give 110 percent" to the job.

Pay scales and the organization of work tasks were a source of constant frustration at Academy. Four teachers—Laura, Dwayne, Sherry, and Travis—were paid hourly wages of between $5 and $6, just above the national minimum wage at that time. Cindy, Marcus, and Rick, salaried workers teaching the core academic curriculum of English, math and history, earned less than $17,000 annually, roughly $6,000 less than first-year teachers working for the local school district on a ten-month calendar. Sherry was still paid less than $18,000 after being promoted to the position of management-level training coordinator, and Ed, the assistant director of the school, was supporting two children in town and paying child support for two others on a salary just over $23,000. There was no formal career ladder or consistent schedule for pay increases or merit bonuses at Academy. The school offered none of the usual job protections that unionization has secured for public school teachers; the director reserved the right, for reasons of student safety, to suspend without pay or to fire any staff person at any time. Moreover, staff had to pass a six-month "trial period" before becoming eligible for employee health benefits. By the director's reasoning, the policy made sense: an Academy job isn't suitable for just anybody, and sometimes it takes new staff members a few trial months to realize they made a mistake.

On top of their classroom duties, all the teachers had been assigned a variety of what might be called "add-on" jobs. Travis, Laura, and Dwayne, for example, served as backup bus drivers and were frequently asked to work at the last minute when regular bus drivers were absent or delayed. Travis was in addition the ad hoc school maintenance man, with duties ranging from fixing jammed toilet valves to painting walls and installing new lighting or door locks. Dwayne's additional assignment was to keep the kitchen cabinets stocked, which meant regular trips to the regional food bank. Rick, in addition to teaching history, had to file and update the federally mandated IEPs. He was the only teacher to receive a free period during the day for this additional assignment.

All the teachers were required to visit students' homes once each month for family conferences. The employee handbook specified that no salaried teacher would receive overtime pay for these visits, even when they had to be conducted at night or on weekends; they were done, perhaps not surprisingly, no more than half as frequently as the official schedule required. Teachers also served as students' homeroom advisors. Ed assigned students to advisors on the basis of where space was available and where a match seemed to him appropriate. Students believed to be "tough" or potentially threatening because of their physical size, especially the boys, were most likely to be assigned to the physically imposing Marcus. Those who spoke Spanish were assigned either to Dwayne or to Laura, both fluent speakers. Girls were assigned mostly to female teachers. Many of the rural students, particularly if they were white, were assigned to Travis. Ed reasoned these were practical choices: they would ease communication between students and staff, encourage the students to regard their teachers as role models, and, he hoped, circumvent what were widely known to be the hesitations of many parents to speak openly in the company of teachers of a race not their own. The result, however, was a certain unevenness in staff advising responsibilities: for all his eagerness, Marcus always seemed to have some particularly demanding students to look after, and usually several more of them than the norm.

Teachers didn't last long on the job. At the beginning of the study, only two of the seven classroom teachers–Dwayne and Laura–had been at Academy for a year or more. By the end, five were gone. Rick disappeared after giving only a day's notice and then reportedly accepted a job in one of the local public middle schools. Despite having a newborn baby at home, Marcus had been asked repeatedly to substitute for an absent bus driver and was being reminded by management almost weekly not to be lax about scheduling home visits. He wrestled with immense personal frustration before leaving Academy to take a job as a teacher in a local district school. Cindy took a brief maternity leave and soon thereafter submitted her resignation. Laura was fired after a series of episodes in which she cried in front of students. Sherry had been scanning the newspapers for job advertisements; not wanting to lose an employee beloved by students and staff, Sean promoted her after less than a year and entered her into a management training program that removed her from daily classroom contact with students; her replacement, a certified teacher brought on at the unprecedented wage rate of $6.50

per hour, stayed little more than five months before taking a higher-paying job elsewhere in the juvenile justice system. Eventually even Sean, the executive director, would be gone.

Academy's contract with the school district called for state-certified teachers. The school, however, was largely unable to attract and keep licensed personnel. Day care, babysitting expenses, and the difficulty of managing personal obligations while also scheduling student home visits, particularly in the many cases where the students' parents worked two jobs or had no phone, were frequent topics of informal conversation among the staff. New staff had to be brought in to replace teachers as they left; the level of experience consequently remained very low, and new hires were placed almost immediately in the classroom. Only one staff member had attended any training program before starting the job. Academy's 71 percent rate of instructional staff turnover during the study far exceeded the state average of 21.5 percent, the district average of 23.4 percent, and the average for the district's alternative-education programs, 20 percent. About 62 percent of teachers employed in the local school district at the time had had four or more years of experience in their jobs. Even among teachers at the local public alternative high schools, 53 percent had had four or more years of teaching, according to state education department statistics. The local school board and superintendent had approved a rule exemption allowing Marcus, Rick, and Cindy to apply for state licenses and enroll in a local district-sponsored teacher-orientation program without having had any of the usual prerequisite training or taking the state licensing examination. They all started the program in late 1995 and were granted two years to complete the necessary college classes, but all left Academy within the year.

The School Building

Built originally as a roadside motel, the Academy building
was a two-story, L-shaped structure set on about two acres
and separated by a narrow creek from its closest neighbors,
a small commercial kennel, a gas station, and a coin laun-
dromat. To the north and east stretched residential neighborhoods of modest single-family homes and apartment
complexes, and to the south a large trailer park, consisting
mostly of rental units, where many of the students and several of the staff members lived. Recent development west of
the school had brought a new county jail, a boot camp for
juvenile felons, and additions to the local community college.

In the building's south wing were a kitchen, an assembly
hall, and three classrooms. The largest room, the assembly
hall, served as the focal point of activity in the school. Bright
underwater scenes of fish and cartoon mermaids painted on
the cinderblock walls endowed the hall with a cheerful,
sunny atmosphere made even sunnier by a row of tall windows that offered, on one side of the room, a panoramic view
of the courtyard lawn with its volleyball net and picnic table.
An American flag dominated the front of the hall, and posted
prominently was a dry-erase board with the names of each
week's top-performing students. Thick wood benches and
tables, pasted with navigational maps of Southern regional
coastlines, were arranged in rows facing the front. Juice and
candy vending machines hummed in the far corner. Students frequently congregated around these, fights breaking
out occasionally over the matter of whose money had gone
into the slot. Eventually, Sean had the candy machine
removed after a particularly serious conflict escalated into
legal charges for one of the students. The adjacent kitchen,

known to staff as "the roach motel," was somewhat minimally equipped with a small refrigerator and an ancient four-burner electric stove caked with grease, which on several occasions caught fire. The padlocked cabinets had been painted a cheerful blue-green color in keeping with the school's prevailing environmental-maritime color scheme.

The classrooms had been carpeted, but the carpeting was soiled and frayed, and the school director convinced a building-contractor friend to remove them. New floor tile installed during the period of my study gave the rooms a fresh if somewhat spartan appearance. Painted white but framed with blue-green paneling, each classroom had the same set of furnishings: a window, a bookcase, a dry-erase board, a bulletin board, a file cabinet, and nine or ten student desks arranged in two or three straight rows facing a larger teacher's desk at the front. Textbooks and workbooks, seven or eight of each, were stacked in neat rows in the bookcases, along with three or four well-worn dictionaries. Like teachers in any school, the staff at Academy had decorated their classrooms to reflect to some degree their individual tastes. Most prominent were the familiar mass-produced school posters; in math and English were portraits of such famous people as Benjamin Franklin and Martin Luther King Jr. (whose teeth someone had scratched out), and all around were myriad computer-generated banners and commercial posters of various sizes and colors bearing motivational slogans: "Go For It!," "Knowledge is Power," and "Education is a Class Act." Cindy, the English teacher, had added handwritten religious announcements: "What you do in the dark will come to light"; "What you are is God's gift to you–What you do is your gift to God." When Rick started his job in late 1995, he blocked the window in the history classroom with a bookcase (to prevent "distractions") and papered the walls with photocopies of state highway maps the students had colored with crayons. The maps remained on the walls for most of the year; they were the school's sole display of student work.

In the east wing were four additional classrooms. One, Travis's woodworking shop, was stocked with a variety of tools, including old machine saws and drill presses. Most of these, handed down from other schools or justice facilities where there had been equipment upgrades, were broken or could not be used because broken saw blades, drill bits, or other necessary supplies had not been replaced or restocked. School administrators talked of their ambition someday to convince a philanthropy or public agency to donate funds for the shop's remodeling. A second vocational classroom was lined with the usual rows of student desks. At the back were about half a dozen outboard motors in various states of disrepair. Intending eventually to include engine repair in the vocational-education curriculum, Sean, ever on the lookout for such supplies, had had these delivered from a nearby state prison where an acquaintance who ran an engine-repair class had no more need for them. The third classroom housed a variety of weights and weightlifting machines; Sherry kept the door open for ventilation, enabling ready access to a volleyball net around the corner in the back of the building as well as a basketball court on asphalt just outside the entrance. The fourth classroom had, in addition to the usual rows of desks and the bulletin board posted with motivational slogans, two fish tanks stocked with small fish and fresh-water shrimp, which Laura had collected from the creek alongside the school. There had been for a short period a turtle in one of the tanks, but students had quietly turned the tank thermostat to its maximum setting one afternoon, essentially boiling the water; Laura had to stay after hours to bleach the equipment. The window to the classroom was blocked with cardboard. At the back, a walk-in closet held wetsuits, oxygen tanks, and other pieces of diving gear. Visitors were usually brought to view these; they were not used by students during the year, however, and the closet remained locked except when visitors came.

Administrative offices clustered at the intersection of the two wings. Through a window in his office, Ed, the assistant director, could monitor noise and movement in the south-wing hallway, and teachers frequently summoned him to the hall by knocking on the glass. There were a staff meeting room and offices for various counselors, community liaisons, and school managers. The receptionist sat in an open cubicle at the front entrance, an area that most likely had once functioned as the motel check-in desk. Upstairs, on the second story, were additional administrative offices, including one belonging to the local juvenile justice case-worker, who because of the proximity could sustain an effectively close watch over the students in her charge. There were also several storage rooms filled with old clothing, couches, and a somewhat haphazard assortment of computer components in various states of repair that had been donated by well-wishers or left by previous occupants of the building. School staff hoped eventually to find someone who could piece together the parts and build a usable computer for the students. In a small upstairs classroom, Dwayne stored the fishing poles and nets for the boating students.

The school owned four canoes, six kayaks, two small single-passenger sailboats, and a 21-foot fishing boat. With the exception of the canoes, which were used almost every week, this equipment was never accessible to students and only idled in a section of the parking lot surrounded by a high chain-link fence. A leaky 26-foot sailboat, lent by another program under the condition that it be repaired, preferably by a student repair crew enrolled in a vocational-education class, sat in a rented dock on the coast; repairs were not attempted during the course of this study.

It can be said that the Academy building was characterized by a conjunction of sparseness and plenty. There were myriad motivational slogans, the prominent posting of the names of high achievers, and what seemed an impressive array of boating and diving gear, evidence of the rewards available for individual achievement, with the blue-green color scheme lending everywhere an optimistic visual coherence. But there also was a distinct paucity of traditional school facilities and materials, and signs at every turn of low social, financial, and academic standing: there were no science, music, or art supplies, no magazine or newspaper subscriptions, and virtually no reading books other than dictionaries and Bibles; the shop equipment was broken; windows had been boarded over in two classrooms; the computers were in fragments in a storage room; the walls, except in one room, were bare of student work. The students were obviously and decidedly needy, physically and emotionally as well as in terms of academic support. School managers made big promises about "saving" them, and staff drew from rich wells of personal concern. Pay scales and a dearth of training and professional development opportunities, however, imposed a certain impoverishment, hinting perhaps at an ambivalence somewhere up the ranks of the system of which the school was a part.

3

The Market System of Merit

ACADEMY'S KEY OPERATIONAL FEATURE was a market-like system of points and ranks exchanged for certain forms of student behavior and agreed to contractually by both students and staff. Token economies, widespread in education as well as in juvenile justice,[1] are touted generally as a humane alternative to more punitive, physical forms of behavior control as well as to more invasive psychotherapies believed somewhat less effective with delinquent children (Greenwood 1988; Greenwood and Zimring 1985; Altschuler and Armstrong 1984). But they are associated, as will be seen, with certain confusions and contradictions.

The Economy of Points and Ranks

Formal entry to the Academy program was initiated no more than two or three days after a student's arrival by the signing of "The Contract," as staff and students referred to it. A several-page document, it specified the classes a student promised to complete (English, math, etc.), the behavioral changes he or she promised to demonstrate ("anger management," "no cursing at parents," "remaining drug free," "obeying curfew"), and the school rules he or she promised to obey in order eventually to prove readiness for graduation. The student, a parent or guardian, and an Academy administrator, usually Ed, the assistant director, all attended the signing, during which students were presented with and asked to study the school handbook listing rules of classroom conduct. There was sober handshaking by all parties.

Students were expected to attain five sequential ranks, or grade levels, during their school stay. New arrivals began at the first, or lowest, rank; after a few weeks they were eligible to progress to the level of second rank; then third, and so on, until they reached the fifth and top rank, from which school graduation was possible. Each rank had its own color, and on special days students were asked to come to school wearing t-shirts, distributed by school staff the day before, of the color signifying their rank in the program. The symbolism of the rank system extended to the spatial organization of the assembly hall; the wooden benches there were arranged in five rows, each row signifying a rank, with the lowest ranking students at the front, nearest to staff watching over them, second-level students behind them, and so on to the rear of the room where the top-ranking students had their own bench farthest from supervising staff, in a symbolic display of their ostensible near-readiness to be released from the most direct and overt staff surveillance. Students often had to be told to "get on the proper bench" when caught wandering off to talk to friends on other benches. Whenever gathering in the assembly hall, students would inspect the back benches to monitor new developments in the rankings. Meritocratic performances were translated in this way into clear visual signage.

To earn rank, students scored points. Points were tallied on small index cards color-coded by rank (plain white for lowest, light blue for second, and so on). After every assembly, meal, and class period, teachers would gather all the point cards and assign scores to each student for that particular meal or time slot, then return the cards to the students for the next period. It was possible to score from 0 to 4 in each of five behavioral categories: "Supervision," which essentially meant staying within sight of a staff member; "Participation," which meant giving "maximum effort" to assignments or work orders; "Attitude/Respect," which boiled down to using acceptable language with supervisors and avoiding making physical or verbal threats to staff or peers; "Leadership," which meant exhibiting overt "helpfulness"; and "Appearance." The five behavioral categories were vague, so the school handbook specified more precise rules. These, many of them picayune, included:

Students may wear a watch, but other jewelry is not permitted.

Males are not allowed to wear earrings.

Cigarettes, lighters, matches, or tobacco products are not allowed.

Radios, walkmans, CD/tape players are not allowed.

Beepers are not permitted in school.

Clothing which advertises tobacco products, alcohol, and drugs or which contains inappropriate language or pictures is not permitted.

Undergarments must not be seen.

Shirts must be tucked in (referring to boys only).

Hats must be worn properly with the bill to the front of the head.

"Ladies" must wear "appropriate" shirts ("no cleavage
showing, no fish nets, etc."), skirts ("no stretch skirts,
no mini skirts, etc."), and undergarments ("slips, bras,
etc.").

Vulgar, abusive, or obscene language or cursing is not
permitted.

Horseplay is not permitted.

Fighting is not permitted.

Acknowledge all staff members and guests . . . with "Sir"
and "Ma'am."

Be polite and courteous to others.

Be quiet and attentive during group meetings.

All females sit in the front of the bus.

Students sit upright and face forward in the seat.

A rule that was not written but nonetheless strictly enforced
through the "Attitude/Respect" category was that students
refer to teachers by "Mr." or "Miss" followed by first name–
a show, in Southern regional dialect, of respect for elders.

If a student scored two points in every category for every
period of the school day, he or she could earn enough points
to reach the top rank and be ready for graduation in about
six months. Fewer points resulted in a longer tenure in the
program; more points could earn an early release.

Students also earned "bonus" points. Noted in the margins
of the index cards, these could be used to "purchase" the
prizes made available every other Friday morning during a
mock auction in the assembly hall. Prizes usually consisted
of cans of soda, bags of candy or potato chips, or meals at
area fast-food outlets. Staff would announce spontaneously
at various points during each week that bonus points would
be offered for a particular task or chore. A teacher having

trouble getting students to do their classwork, for example, might announce that she would grant bonus points to anyone willing to search the dictionary for vocabulary words and copy their definitions (for example: "thirty points per definition"). If the assembly hall garbage can was particularly full after lunch, a staff member might offer bonus points to two or three students willing to take the can to the dumpster outside. Occasionally, students earned bonus points for shaking hands or offering friendly greetings to important visitors, for example legislators or state agency inspectors. An entire class of students earned several hundred bonus points each one hot day when they agreed to sit quietly in a sweltering classroom where there was no air conditioning.

To add force to the point system, student names were posted on a chart in the assembly hall on Fridays indicating the number of points each student had acquired for the week. Friday afternoons were "rec" time, with the usual class schedule partly replaced by fishing trips, movies, bowling, or lunches at area fast-food outlets. In a lunchtime assembly held every Friday, highest-scoring students got to choose the rec activity they preferred. Middle-scoring students chose from among the offerings left over. Lowest-scoring students had to remain in the building and attend their regular classes. This latter feature of the rewards system, with the lowest scorers required to stay in class, acknowledged student and staff conceptions of schoolwork as drudgery; it enforced within the classroom social system the broader cultural separation of labor ("going to class") from leisure ("rec").

"Consequences" were the punishment for certain rule violations, essentially a period of forced labor on a school work crew. Students received "consequences" for such violations as skipping school, walking defiantly out of class, cursing particularly intensely on the bus or in class, engaging in fist-fights, getting caught with cigarettes, or if they were found to have been away from home past the 9:00 curfew the night before when the school monitor visited or phoned. Most days, a staff member was specially designated as the "consequences supervisor"; this job was taken over on a full-time basis by Sherry after her promotion to management. At least three students–and sometimes as many as ten–would be assigned to work crews on any given day. This usually meant having to mow the schoolyard lawn, wash the vans, rake the flowerbeds, sweep or mop the hallways and lunchroom, or scrub graffiti from walls or desktops. One eight-month-pregnant girl who violated her evening curfew order was asked the next day to file papers in the school office. In the summer, when the air conditioning sometimes broke and classrooms steamed, a few students tried deliberately–and usually successfully–to get themselves on work crews: they walked out of class, cursed at staff, or made ostentatious displays of their illicit stashes of cigarettes or their personal cassette recorders.

Like the point system of which they were a part, consequences were structured along the lines of a market economy, appearing as deals freely entered by logical and responsible agents, with rough equivalence taken to exist among the commodities being exchanged. A day's raking or several hours of filing were the price of a night out carousing, a mowed lawn could be exchanged for a package of cigarettes, an afternoon wiping desktops for an episode of cursing at a teacher. The consequence system represented an institutional cost savings as well: the school had no regular custodial or lawn maintenance services; disruptive students could be assigned the duties for which ordinary public schools hired salaried staff.

Students in work crews missed class time and therefore earned no points during their punishment. This could mean an extra day tacked onto their tenure in the program. High scores one day being compensation for low scores the next, the consequence system sometimes encouraged students who were disruptive to seek, at specific times, high scores in classes and assemblies.

In case the point and consequence systems didn't discourage rule violations, students were also searched periodically for contraband—no more than three times a week and usually only once every few weeks. Searches usually took place in the morning before breakfast. A female staff member would lead the girls one by one into a bathroom and examine their pants, dress, or shirt pockets. The boys would be lined up in a classroom, asked to empty their pockets, and frisked in view of the group by a male staff member who also examined socks and sleeves. Items typically found during searches included electronic pagers and small cassette players, cigarettes, and cigarette lighters. On two occasions students were found with cocaine; several students were found during the year with marijuana; one boy was caught hiding a stolen gun in a jacket pocket. For such serious infractions, the police would be called, and everyone would take in the somber tableau of a classmate being led off to booking.

When they wanted to move up in rank, students submitted a form on which they noted their point scores and listed any specific achievements (completing all the work for a particular course, for example, or passing an entire month without assignment to a work crew) rendering them eligible for promotion. The staff deliberated once every two weeks behind closed doors, usually on Thursdays during breakfast or morning assembly, to decide who could progress to the next level. Deliberations were called "hearings." Students seeking promotion would be called in one by one to make brief statements about their accomplishments.

Organizational Features Supporting the Market System of Merit

The school day was ordered in a way that offered students the opportunity to win points. Vans carrying the students arrived in the parking lot between 8:30 and 9 A.M., at which point students would file out and proceed to their benches in the assembly hall. Breakfast was not a part of the official budget or program, but Sean, health-conscious since his days as a competitive weightlifter, made sure it was always provided, served usually by Cindy or Sherry. Students arrived at school obviously hungry most days, many having had no dinner the night before. The school supplied plastic cups and spoons, fresh milk, and occasionally apples or oranges. Boxed cereals were purchased in bulk from the regional food bank, where supermarkets and restaurants donated foods nearing or past their expiration dates. Trix or Fruit Loops were the usual fare, never fresh but always devoured extremely eagerly. On Fridays there were doughnuts, and on special assembly days, roughly once a month except during the summer, Marcus, the math teacher, volunteered to come to school early (without pay) to scramble eggs and fry pancakes in the school kitchen as an extra treat, much appreciated, for the students.

When all the vans were in, the students seated, and breakfast distributed, one student would be chosen, usually by Ed, to lead the group in the call-and-response breakfast-time prayer:

"God is good," the student would announce. The group in unison would then repeat: "God is good."

"God is great," the student would say.

"God is great," came the group's response.

"Let us thank him."

"Let us thank him."

"For this plate."

"For this plate."

Officially secular, with no religious affiliation, and subject formally to the usual regulations concerning the separation of church and state that governed other city schools and educational facilities, Academy was nonetheless imbued with religious imagery and references, as will be seen. Christian prayer was a part of daily school life, for students and for teachers.

Breakfast lasted fifteen or twenty minutes, during which the van drivers reported to the front office any problems they had encountered on the morning rounds. Teachers generally joined the students for morning meal, sitting among them at the benches. It was a time for relaxed and cheerful conversation before the start of the official school day.

At the end of the morning meal, Ed would announce homeroom, and the students would line up with their assigned advisors, who led them out of the assembly hall to their classrooms. Homeroom didn't last more than five or ten minutes; it was mostly a transitional period. Students would take seats and talk quietly among themselves, most of them still sleepy. Neighborhood news was the favored topic: who'd been arrested the night before and for what, who'd thrown a party, which police officers had been on the beat, who was in the hospital. Teachers called for quiet if they heard cursing, arguing, or talk of drugs or alcohol. Some of the students browsed idly through newspapers if these were available. Cindy used the time, most days, to copy biblical quotations onto little sheets of looseleaf paper and distribute them among the students. Marcus sometimes passed a Bible around his classroom; he also kept handy a small paperback about famous African Americans. Laura stored in her desk drawer a paperback book of quotations, which she would pass around her homeroom along with sheets of looseleaf paper and pencils so students could copy the entries.

Morning assembly period came next. Assemblies were held every day, once in the morning following homeroom and then again in the afternoon following fifth-period classes. On Fridays there was an additional assembly at lunchtime. Assemblies almost always followed the same routine and were regarded by students and staff alike as a good opportunity to score points. The homeroom teachers would bring the students from the classrooms back to the assembly hall and send them to their benches. Staff would gather at the front of the room or line up along the sides. One staff member, usually Ed, would then take a position at the front; he would thank students for coming to school and announce any special plans for the day, such as whether visitors would be in the building or if there were going to be unusual changes to the schedule. Ed would then ask the group for volunteers to raise their hands to lead the Lord's Prayer. Hands would go up from among the benches; one would be selected. "Our father," the student would begin, and then others would join in unison:

> Who art in heaven, hallowed be thy name. Thy kingdom come, they will be done, on earth as it is in heaven. Give us this day our daily bread, and forgive us our trespasses, as we

forgive those who trespass against us. Lead us not into temptation, but deliver us from Evil. God's is the kingdom, the power and glory. Amen.

The teachers would then make their way among the seated students, gathering the point cards. Throughout assembly period, staff would observe the students and note scores for each in the point cards. Students leading the Lord's Prayer scored at least three points, sometimes four, in the "Participation" and "Leadership" categories for that period.

After "Prayer" came the flag pledge. "Pledge," Ed would announce. A few students' hands would go up. One would be chosen. The student would stand and begin: "I pledge allegiance to the flag," followed by the others reciting in unison: "of the United States of America . . ." Pledge would be followed by vigorous applause by students and staff, who then continued with their scoring of the point cards. Handclapping insured for students a score of two in the "Participation" category.

Then Ed would call: "Word for the Day." A few hands would go up; four or five would be selected. "Word" was a recitation of dictionary definitions or brief slogans, usually taken from among the ones posted on the classroom walls. Among the most frequent offerings: "Leadership: the act of being a leader," "Respect: showing respect for others," "Knowledge is power," and "Responsibility: taking responsibility for your actions." More intense clapping would follow.

Then the call: "Safety Tip." More hands up, more volunteers chosen. Safety tips offered most frequently: "Buckle up," "Don't drink and drive," "Wear a life jacket when you're in the water," "Just say no to drugs." Then more vigorous clapping, accompanied by more scoring of the point cards.

This was followed by "Current Event." Hands up; volunteers chosen. Students would stand and offer personal announcements ("Today is my birthday") or, more commonly, brief clips from the morning's news headlines ("The Braves won"; "A man got killed but they caught the guy that did it."). Again, vigorous applause would follow, and then the call would come: "Positive Thought." More hands up; more volunteers chosen. Frequent offerings: "What you do in the dark will come to light"; "If the world gives you lemons, make lemonade." Occasionally students at this point would read the scriptural quotations Cindy or Marcus had suggested for them back in homeroom ("He who has no dreams shall perish," for example), or a line from the quotation book provided by Laura for this purpose.

Assembly performances made for occasional irony: students in the back of the room often clapped when they couldn't hear what was being said in the front. Though some Academy students had parents in prison, there was vigorous applause the day a volunteer announced for "Current Events" that chain gangs had been reinstated in the state prisons. Occasionally, a teacher standing on the sidelines would throw small pieces of candy (Tootsie Rolls, for instance) to the benches of the students who were volunteering for assembly; participation on such days tended to reach particularly high levels.

Morning roll call would follow, an auditory string of "Here, Sir's". Then came a brief motivational speech by assistant director Ed, usually exhorting students to "do all your classwork," "be respectful of students and staff," "be thankful for what you got," or remember that "the time we leave this afternoon will depend on your attitude and respect." At the end, the students would be dismissed to first-period classes.

Afternoon assemblies followed the morning-assembly format, with staff at the front or along the sides of the room and

students arranged on their benches. In the afternoons, however, instead of "Current Event" and "Pledge" and so on, students were required to report "Positives," favorable things
they had accomplished at school that day. A typical offering:
"I woke up, went to class, did my work, and had a great day."
In addition, staff were expected to "give Staff Positives" after
the students had finished. Ed, or whoever was running the
afternoon assembly, would call out teachers' names to
receive their responses. A typical Staff Positive: "I had a great
day. I saw students making progress on their respect levels
and leadership. Keep it up." These were followed always by
vigorous applause from the group. The afternoon prayer,
recited in unison by the whole of the assembly, was:

> May the Lord watch between me and Thee, while we're
> absent one from the other. This we ask, in Jesus' name,
> Amen.

Students would then be lined up to board the vans for the
ride home.

A few students, usually no more than three or four,
remained in the building for an after-school period that
extended the school day to 6:30 or 7:00 P.M. Run by part-
timers who had little contact with the regular teachers, the
after-school program took in students in the first few weeks
after admission, a time when it was believed they were most
prone to commit new crimes and in need of the greatest
amount of supervision. On a typical afternoon, staff cooked
hotdogs and canned beans or microwaved macaroni and
cheese in the school kitchen and then took the students on
brief bowling trips, to the movies, or to the library. To leave
the after-school program and resume the normal school
schedule, students first had to earn five hundred sixty points;

at the end they were assigned one high school credit for a life skills class accredited through the local school district.

The market system derived support not just from the ordering of the school day, with its multiple assemblies and opportunities for point-score acquisition, but also from the physical organization of the building and student movement through it, and from the scheduling of frequent communication among the staff. Small classrooms, for example, enabled the continuous surveillance of students by teachers, a component of the program touted by school officials as the most effective and humane way to prevent students from wandering off campus even in the absence of locks and bars. For part of the year, until all the devices had either broken or disappeared, some of the teachers carried walkie-talkies so they could summon the assistant director when fights erupted or seemed imminent. Radios in the school vans enabled continuous communication between van drivers and the receptionist's office. Standing in the doorways of their classrooms, teachers could supervise students' short-distance travel to bathrooms, and students moving the short distances to classes or assemblies were arranged into single-file lines flanked by teachers in a ratio of no more than seven or eight students to a staff member. This system was not foolproof: students on occasion wandered off campus. Police found one girl hiding in the creek near the school, huddled in a spot where the banks formed a narrow ditch.

The monitoring of physical activity replayed itself at several levels: the window linking the main first-floor administrative suite to the south-wing hallway enabled management to keep an eye on teachers' efforts to keep their classes quiet. Moreover, the school director maintained an "open door" visitation policy; with numerous government offices relatively nearby, the building received a steady stream of curious onlookers, and few weeks passed without an official visit of some kind from college students, municipal or law enforcement officials, state agency supervisors, or legislators representing a variety of criminal justice and finance committees. Top-performing students got to serve as tour guides–a coveted assignment, since it represented students' only legitimate time out of direct staff view.

Teachers documented and coordinated their scrutiny of students not just hourly through the point card system, but also daily, weekly, monthly, and at other intervals through staff meetings and on a wide variety of lists and official forms. Every morning before students arrived, the teachers would meet briefly in a classroom where Ed would report the major events of the previous night–which students had violated curfew, for instance; which, if any, had been arrested; what family feuds had erupted and with what results. Staff also met every afternoon, if only for ten or fifteen minutes, after the students left. Though many of the nonteaching staff were out of the building much of the time, usually in court or paying visits to families or probation officers, they sustained daily contact with teachers and administrators by attending these brief afternoon meetings. Each week, moreover, usually during the afternoon staff meeting, teachers wrote a sentence or two about each student on what was called a Behavioral Progress Report. There were also monthly Student Update forms submitted to the juvenile court judge. Monthly minicontracts listing "goals for the month" were supposed to be completed as well, preferably collectively by students, staff, and parents during each month's home visit. (Usually, they were filled out by teachers themselves, sometimes after brief conversations with students in class.)

Teachers also submitted lesson plans each week for the education director (although these were not taken at all seriously by either party, as will be seen), and every nine weeks grades for each student had to be submitted to the local school district administrator. Monthly, teachers submitted separate grade sheets for senior students being evaluated for graduation readiness. Moreover, for students enrolled as a transition from higher-level treatment programs, teachers every hour were supposed to fill out Behavior Checklists, answering such questions as "Was the student's attitude acceptable?" and "Did the student respect others' property?" Even off hours, all staff members had to carry report forms on which to describe any encounters with the students outside school–if while driving across town, for example, they happened on a student near a crack house or in the company of some person or gang the student was supposed to be avoiding. Surveillance and monitoring of students in line with the contract system was in this way made virtually continuous, highly formal, extremely labor intensive, and always "on the record."

History and Contradictions of the Market System of Merit

Pervasive in the school, starting with the signing of the contract and reinforced daily through the point cards, bonus points, and consequence system, was a metaphor of market and exchange, of people entering into deals and negotiating transactions. But the market system presented several contradictions. On one hand, formal rules regarding punishment and reward reinforced a prevailing theme of trade and exchange, of merit duly rewarded and misdeeds repaid in kind. Market metaphors pointed to fairness and freedom of a certain kind, to students' ability to choose their own actions and their capacity, as logical, responsible agents, to accept the known consequences of their choices. Contracts, as sociologist Emile Durkheim (1984) noted, include beneath the surface certain definitions of the people who enter into them and what legitimately can be asked of them. A contract says of a person that he or she is trustworthy enough to enter into formal agreements. For Academy's students—many of them accustomed to being publicly berated by teachers and police and regarded by the public as mentally or morally deficient and undeserving of trust—the school's contracts conceded humanity, granted autonomy, announced the possibility that even lawbreakers can make a deal and stick to it.

On the other hand, contracts and points called for a great deal of restraint. To sign the contract agreeing to follow Academy rules—to sit when the school handbook specified, to wear hats in a particular way, to renounce certain styles of jewelry or clothing, and to participate with a show of eagerness in sometimes bizarre ceremonies in the assembly hall—was to allow that the rules were legitimate and that teachers had authority to enforce them. In exchange for being granted stature as responsible contract-signing agents, the students conceded school authority over minute details of their daily movements and actions. Freed, by the fact of having signed a contract, from some of the hurtful psychological stereotypes associated with delinquency, students were tethered by the very same contract to picayune regulations and conventions they had had no part in making and about which they were allowed no comment.

The market system of merit has its antecedents in an early nineteenth-century methodological convergence of educational and penal management. Two large state penitentiaries were built in the United States after the Revolutionary War that represented two differing philosophies of punishment and conceptions of crime and criminals. One, in Philadelphia, was a castle-like structure where convicts were locked in solitary confinement, exercised in isolated courtyards, and, it was intended, reflected quietly on their legal and moral violations (Erikson 1968; Rothman 1980). Since inmates were kept apart, fights very seldom broke out; there was little need for discipline. Prison authorities touted the arrangement as an alternative to the physical brutality and inconsistency of early colonial justice and as a model of humane and nonviolent practice that led to long-term reformation of souls. The second penitentiary, at Auburn, New York, stressed group activity rather than solitude. Large numbers of inmates worked together at hard labor in tightly supervised gangs, sometimes contracted out to local industries. They ate in a common mess hall, attended classes as a group, and were marched collectively from station to station. Advocates hailed the system as an alternative to the inhumane loneliness imposed by solitary confinement. But to maintain order under crowded conditions, prison officials enforced a policy of absolute silence among their charges; moreover, they made liberal use of the whip. The Philadelphia system, the product of Quaker thinking, embodied architecturally and managerially a commitment to personal reformation through religious meditation. Key to the Auburn model, on the other hand, was the discipline and constant surveillance of the guards. Prisoners at Auburn experienced physically the Puritan religious conviction that criminals had to be broken and habituated to acceptable behavioral routines (Erikson 1968).

The behavioral system at Auburn soon came to dominate American penology.[2] It was relatively inexpensive and easily transferable to other sites. Pedagogical rather than punitive, its goal was to train the most recalcitrant, through drill and practice, to do what was asked of them. The new system decoupled behavior from beliefs, the public life of the body from the private life of the mind—replaying inside the prison the separation of public from private spheres that was increasingly characterizing social life outside the prison. "Perhaps, leaving the prison," wrote French observers Alexis de Tocqueville and Gustave de Beaumont, who toured the United States in 1831:

> the former convict . . . is not an honest man, but he has contracted honest habits[;] . . . if he is not more virtuous, he has become at least more judicious. . . . His religious faith is perhaps neither lively nor deep; but even supposing that religion has not touched his heart, his mind has contracted habits of order. . . . Finally, if he has not become in truth, better, he is at least more obedient to the laws, and that is all which society has a right to demand. (de Beaumont and de Tocqueville 1964, 59–60)

A second important development in penal practice appeared with the opening of the Elmira Penitentiary in New York State in 1877. Built in the wake of investigations of prison brutality in the older facilities, Elmira embodied a liberal reformism aimed specifically at youthful prisoners. All its inmates were under age thirty, and its key feature was the indeterminate sentence. Indeterminate sentencing meant that judges assigned lawbreakers to prison without setting the dates of ultimate release. Rather, front-line prison staff would determine release dates based on what they perceived to be a prisoner's readiness to enter community life. To measure readiness with consistency and, it was hoped, rationality, Elmira's managers deployed the now well-known system of ranks and points by which to grade each prisoner's performance. Starting his confinement at grade two, a prisoner could fulfill work and study assignments, committing no disciplinary infractions, and thereby earn, in time, enough points to move up to the next level. Eventually, he would reach the grade level from which release was possible. Troublesome inmates could be demoted, and each rank had an associated array of privileges as well as a distinctly colored uniform. Inmate performances on academic work and maintenance chores were central to the grading and scoring system; it was assumed, by a certain leap in logic, that meritocratic performances inside the institution were a good indicator of how a prisoner would behave on the outside (Rothman 1980; Dumm 1987). Supporters believed that indeterminate sentencing would be humane and equitable, replacing physical violence with a more gentle and indirect pressure on inmates to obey prison rules (Platt 1969).

The major precedent for Elmira's innovations had come from the educator Joseph Lancaster, whose ideas had profoundly influenced school management trends earlier in the century. In the schools he founded for children of the poor, Lancaster had taken the bold and unprecedented step of abolishing the traditional schoolmaster's whip. In its place he established a highly bureaucratic system of promotions and merit badges distributed on the basis of "inspections" and competitive "examinations." Lancaster organized children for the first time into what today are called "classes"; if they wanted to move up through the class ranks, they had, as in the outside world of work, to perform to specifications in behavior and in academic work and impress their supervisors with performances of compliant diligence and industry (Spring 1990; Kaestle 1983; Katz 1968). The system emphasized submission, orderliness, consistency, and rationality as well as humane treatment and low administrative costs. Educators of the period drew strong analogies between the new method of schooling and the factory system, where hard work, systematically measured, earned ostensibly just and predictable rewards. Lancaster's introduction into the classroom of meritocratic principles was the pedagogical expression, as historian David Hogan (1989) has noted, of that era's broader market revolution; it brought schools in line with an emerging modern cultural economy.

For both prisons and schools, indeterminate sentencing, grading, and the rank and point systems were tools stronger in some respects than the old-fashioned whip. Since they seemed to require a kind of internalized self-discipline on the part of inmates and students, with overt physical violence replaced by a far quieter but still forceful psychological coercion, they didn't inspire crusading investigations of brutality or complaints of excessive harshness. Rather, they made obedience seem like a rational, responsible choice. Though investigations not long after Elmira's founding revealed inmate beatings little different from those prevailing at less reform-minded facilities, and though punishments at Lancaster's schools took on a character as crude as those at any traditional school, the new management strategies had long-lasting effects. But their fundamental contradiction remains: when schooling becomes a feature of sentencing, the lines between education and punishment are ambiguous, as both students and staff at Academy were well aware. What goes by the name education can itself seem like punishment.

Neither wholly prison-like nor wholly school-like, hinting at incapacitation as well as empowerment, at impoverishment as well as riches, Academy offered both rewards and punishments, freedoms and unfreedoms. Having inherited methodologies from education and juvenile casework, the students and staff at Academy suffered, not surprisingly, from their long-standing tensions. In the market system, freedom was accompanied by unfreedom, a certain kind of empowerment by reminders that authority emanates from above. Moreover, all market exchanges were encumbered, as perhaps market exchanges always are, by larger relations of power–by the ever-looming threat of longer captivity or transfer to a more punitive and far less desirable "higher-end" treatment program. Students could walk off campus, since no fence was secure and no gate kept locked; they could, if they wanted, bring guns into the building or choose to accept zeroes on their point cards. But school failure here sometimes meant boot camp or even prison. Police could arrive at any time to haul a misbehaving classmate to the regional detention center.

4

Curriculum Units of Exchange

THERE ARE ONLY SO MANY WAYS to organize learning in tiny rooms managed by teachers with minimal training and experience and full of sometimes bitter and hostile students of diverse skill levels, some of whom are getting very little sleep and each of whom starts school at a unique point in the year and according to a schedule over which school staff have no control. Academy staff relied heavily in this context on schooling's traditional twentieth-century technologies: the ditto, the worksheet, and the fill-in-the-blank sentence. In history, math, English, and oceanography, the curriculum was organized into what were called "units"– stapled-together sets of photocopied worksheets or single-page lists of short written exercises, some matched to workbooks or textbooks housed on classroom shelves. A division of academic course content into minute tasks students could complete in short time periods, sometimes only three or four minutes, units were the basis of what school managers called "individualized instruction," the theory being that students could complete units at their own pace.

Soon after Academy opened its doors, a representative had met with the school district's dropout prevention supervisor;

they'd hammered out an agreement by which particular packages of units would be defined as the equivalent of a standard public school class. In this way, Academy courses were regarded administratively as ordinary high school classes, each could be matched to a course reference number in the school district's master list, and documentation could be made (there was a special skills-checklist form for this purpose) of the state-mandated skills that students enrolled in the courses had ostensibly mastered by the fact of having completed their units. This system was the practical basis of the school district's approach to quality control of the Academy program: with course materials standardized into unit packets, student achievement readily measurable in terms of number of packets completed, and skills acquisition reportable on a simple checklist, administrators at the school district and at Academy could report specific instructional outcomes, the kind of bottom-line data sought by oversight boards, taxpayer organizations, and legislative committees. It can be said in this sense that the unit-based organization of the curriculum was driven at least in part by political currents.

Each class consisted of a distinct number of units. English I, for example, consisted of forty-seven units. History consisted of five, with multiple worksheets in each. Oceanography had seven units, each consisting of six or seven worksheets, supplemented ostensibly by three or four associated hands-on "laboratory" or "field" assignments. Math followed a textbook, with each chapter a unit. Each student was assigned a file folder in every classroom for storing his or her unit work. The photocopied sheets making up the units were mostly shared among the entire school, each teacher maintaining only a limited quantity of them, so students were not allowed to write on them.

For many young people in American schools, the annual August or September ritual of buying classroom supplies holds special pleasures, anxieties, and symbolism: students take a few minutes before school starts to imagine themselves as craftspeople of a certain type, bearing backpacks or pencil holders of a particular color, shape, or design, signifying some allegiance or identity and the authority to possess one's own work tools. But Academy students did not bring their own pencils, notebooks, or other traditional supplies to school, since handbags and backpacks, potential concealment for drugs or weapons, were not permitted. Instead, the school provided the essential materials. On entering class, students would be directed to a file cabinet to retrieve a unit. Then they were handed or took for themselves a pencil and one or two sheets of looseleaf paper from the stacks teachers maintained on their desks. Everything had to be written on the looseleaf paper provided. Pencils were to be returned at the end of the period. If a student needed a textbook or workbook to complete the unit, he or she could retrieve one for the period from the bookcase. Classes started always this same way: students wrote the date and unit number in the top right-hand corner of their looseleaf sheets.

Unit work was uniformly rote and mechanical.[1] In English I, a course in which virtually all students enrolled, having failed or missed it in high school, the vast majority of units consisted of sparse and brief drills in elementary-level grammar, spelling, and copying. The students had to circle nouns, underline verbs, rewrite one-line sentences using semicolons or the correct forms of pronouns, or copy from textbooks or dictionaries the definitions of vocabulary words or parts of speech. There were a few reading and writing assignments, mostly "short-answer" exercises requiring, in practice, no more than two sentences. In math, with one or two exceptions, students were enrolled in a remedial "pre-algebra" course with a textbook stressing elementary arithmetic.

In oceanography, where the units had been derived from a curriculum guide designed by the state department of education for use in alternative schools, there was a great deal of vocabulary work, with long lists of words the definitions of which had to be looked up in classroom dictionaries. There were also "word search" games and crossword puzzles. Not permitted to write on their unit worksheets, however, since these were shared among the entire student body, students had to list their answers to crossword clues in columns on their looseleaf papers. Brief fill-in-the-blank or complete-the-sentence exercises required students to read a few stapled-together worksheet pages and then copy selected words or phrases exactly as they had appeared in the original text. Students rarely did even these rudimentary readings, however; they mostly scanned the pages briefly in search of the paragraphs harboring the correct words or word sequences. Some of the worksheets were ragged and dog-eared from having been used dozens of times; in a few of them, the correct words or phrases had already been underlined by previous readers so that even scanning was unnecessary. On one unit worksheet requiring students to label parts of a diagram depicting the water cycle (precipitation, evaporation, condensation), the teacher had already filled in the labels so that students had merely to copy the words onto their looseleaf sheets. According to the state-issued curriculum guidebook that accompanied the units and was stored in the classroom bookcase, the worksheets were intended only as a supplement to class discussions and hands-on laboratory or field exercises; the skills checklist form approved by the school district, accordingly, called for a series of field measurements using real marine specimens. Academy students fulfilled this requirement in class by using rulers to measure the length and width of large metal bolts and screws stored in a jar in the teacher's desk drawer. "Pretend this is a fish," is how Laura introduced these assignments when distributing the rulers and bolts to her students. There were no class discussions of marine biology.

Rick, the history teacher, had started the job with a great deal of enthusiasm. Determined to make the curriculum more rigorous and exciting, he developed several unorthodox class projects for which Sean eagerly set aside funds. Rick brought crayons to school, first of all, so that the students could color state highway maps. He also brought in map puzzles and a timer; with these he aimed to foster healthy competition over geographical knowledge. Later, he rented from the public library a set of videotapes of the 1970s television series "Roots," the saga of a black family's struggle through slavery and the Civil War. His most ambitious project was an "ethnic cooking" unit on regional native and immigrant cultures: learning about Native Americans, students broiled fish and corn in the school kitchen; commemorating European settlement, they boiled beef and egg noodles; beans and rice represented Caribbean immigration. Rick intended to supplement the cooking with some readings about immigration. With no resources on hand at the school, however, and little time left to search the public library after conducting the required student home visits, he took what was readily available from home; students received as worksheets several photocopied excerpts from the popular 1990 cookbook *The Frugal Gourmet on Our Immigrant Ancestors,* such as: "Cuban immigrants have a very low rate of unemployment and a very high median annual income, and at least half of the Cuban Americans have graduated from high school[;] . . . they are often marked as 'foreigners' when in reality they are committed Americans" (Smith 1990). Rick encountered other snags in his efforts as well: when some other city resident borrowed from the library one of the videotapes from the "Roots" series, Rick had to show his class an incomplete version of the story.

Rick had arranged it so that in addition to getting the usual points for "Attitude," "Participation," "Leadership," and so on, students were graded during hands-on work for what he termed "Class Cooperation," with scores tabulated for each student in such matters as willingness to wash dishes or attentiveness to class video presentations. Rick's brother-in-law had given him an old computer; he kept it in his classroom to print out the tabulation forms he designed for this purpose. Cooperation scores were subsequently "averaged in" to other grades for the unit of which the project was a component. Even unorthodox projects, in essence, were tailored to fit within the system of units and points.

Rick also developed a unit on religion in state history. For this he incorporated a workbook published by a think tank affiliated with the Moral Majority, the right-wing religious organization. Students read that the Declaration of Independence "marked the birth of this nation which, under God, was destined for world leadership" and that "The Constitution was designed to perpetuate a Christian order." They were instructed that the country's "moral fabric had been woven with the durable threads of Scriptural truth" and that "Those who today would secularize America destroy the nation's very heritage." Drawing from the readings, Rick designed his own set of unit worksheets: students filled in blanks from such sentences as "The freedom of the first amendment from federal interference is not _____ (correct answer: "from") religion but _____ (correct answer: "for") religion in the constituent states." Rick said one day: "The school district would not like what I'm doing here, but I think these kids need it."

At the end of each class period, students would file their looseleaf sheets in their assigned folders, which then went back into the file cabinets or, in some cases, were presented to the teacher as evidence that unit work had actually been completed that day. An exchange was effected: handing in their looseleaf sheets, students received in return their point cards, updated with the scores for that period.

Rick and Laura tended to grade unit papers on the spot, marking "incorrect" items with an "X" and then tallying the unit score where possible. Laura sometimes tallied "correct" items with a checkmark and returned looseleaf sheets for revision if more than a fourth of responses were incorrect, but neither teacher offered much in the way of explanation or commentary. "Fix this" was the dominant remark. Cindy and Marcus, by contrast, did little in-class grading at all for about five months; they computed grades for student papers all at once in one long cram session a day or two before nine-week progress reports were due at the public school district office. In some cases they didn't mark the papers at all, instead assigning "A," "B," or "C" on the district roll sheet based on general suspicions of what students had actually accomplished. "We don't have a lot of time to do all that grading," Cindy said. After considerable prodding from the education director, Kevin–who almost daily asked, "Got any grades for me?"–and just before the arrival of investigators from the state juvenile justice agency, who were conducting their annual inspection of the program, Cindy and Marcus started spending class time actually scoring student papers. Behavior report forms, which they had been finishing in class, had subsequently to be done during unpaid overtime after school or at home. Marcus eventually typed and posted in his classroom an instruction sheet directing students to check their own papers using the answer keys in the appendix of their textbooks. Not surprisingly, this was interpreted by students as an opportunity essentially to copy the answers from the book without even glancing at the problems.

Students regarded their unit work with something less than enthusiasm. Entering their classrooms at the start of each class period, some students would make a point of remembering the units they had completed previously and would retrieve new ones roughly in numerical order. At least an equal number, however, simply reached into the file cabinet without looking and settled for whatever came out first. Sometimes students grabbed a handful of unit worksheets and passed them out among their friends. Apathy toward the content of the units was a feature of all academic classes. It was not unusual to find in student folders evidence that some units had been completed several times over or, more likely, started several times on various occasions but never actually finished. This was particularly the case among the seventeen- and eighteen-year-olds. Many were so behind in their school careers, several years below grade in terms of academic performance yet over age by at least a year and oftentimes more, that they expected never to return successfully to an ordinary public school; they consequently saw little reason to work toward the traditional credits available through the unit system. The same was true for the younger students who had been expelled: most expected that regardless of what happened at Academy, they would be funneled eventually to the local public alternative high school for delinquent teens, a place universally despised among the students because of its reputation for harsh discipline. The outcome appeared the same whether they completed credits or not.

The primary classroom task, in this context, was not so much actually to complete academic work and thereby earn credit for learning, but rather merely to do whatever was necessary in order to garner the behavioral points, rewards, and rank increases that could buy release from the program. Behaving or appearing busy–earning thereby a score of at least two in the "Participation" and "Attitude" sections of the point cards–became at least as important as actually being busy. Reinforced within the heart of classroom organization were the very themes that prevailed in the school's physical layout, assembly programs, and overall behavior management scheme–the themes of buying and selling, of a market where performances of certain types could be exchanged for points and rank increases in a transaction between deliberate actors. There was no group instruction. Direct instruction of any type was both rare and unnecessary, since much of the unit work was rudimentary and self-contained, requiring little engagement with higher-level concepts or principles. Teachers virtually never attempted to visit students at their desks.

Brokering, Fighting, Recreation: Three Variations on Classroom Climate

Among the teachers there were three distinct classroom styles, each associated with a distinct classroom climate. Two teachers, Marcus and Cindy, took what might be characterized as a brokering approach to classroom market transactions; they made few comments in class, paid attention mostly to their own paperwork at their own desks, and allowed students, within certain limits, to pace their own work, napping when they wanted to or taking time out for personal grooming or quiet private conversations with friends. Both teachers reinforced the market-like nature of classroom transactions by focusing their attention and comments not on matters of substantive academic content but almost exclusively on issues of classroom management. Praise and rewards were given to students who appeared busy and remained relatively quiet but were not necessarily completing assignments. Responses to student questions centered on sustaining classroom quiet and student compliance. When on occasion the classrooms became noisy enough potentially to attract attention from hallway passers-by, both teachers called for silence, recalled point-system policy, or prodded students to tend to their units. "It's too loud in here. You should be doing your work, not talking," was a common refrain. The following illustrate typical exchanges.

LaTeesha is working on an English unit. There are six students in the room, one sleeping with his head down on the desk and the rest sitting and talking among themselves in a relaxed manner, tending to their units every few minutes. Cindy is leafing through a stack of paperwork on her desk. LaTeesha will soon be coming up for a promotion in rank; she is determined to finish several units each day of the week until she completes the entire course. The assignment before her, Unit 18, is about biographic poetry. It requires nine short lines of verse, and the instructions offer prompts for each line: "Line 1:

[Write] Your first name only; Line 2: [Write] Four adjectives that describe you; Line 3: "Sibling of or son/daughter of . . ." and so on. LaTeesha gets stuck on Line 2. She asks out loud: "What you supposed to do?" Looking up briefly from her desk, Cindy replies: "Just follow the instructions and do the work." LaTeesha soon finishes the assignment on her own, going on eventually to complete all the units in the course within a few weeks.

Edwin, a seventeen-year-old, is working on a math unit about decimals. The workbook instructions give him three numbers—14, 14.2, and 13.9—which he needs to arrange in order from lowest to highest. He asks Marcus out loud: "How do I do this?" From his desk, Marcus has Edwin read the question out loud. He then goes to the dry-erase board, writing the correct answer and explaining, "You put the 14 in the middle because you look at what comes after the decimal point and that tells you." Edwin nods and copies the numbers from the board. Marcus says, "Good work. Keep it up."

Two students in math have workbooks closed on their desks. One is tapping a ruler on his hands; the other, apparently about to lose an infected fingernail, is alternately inspecting his hands and trying to nap with his head down. Two other students seem to be writing. One is meticulously copying the unit questions from the textbook onto her looseleaf sheet but not actually answering any of them. "Good work," Marcus says, referring to her by name. The other is muttering to himself, hunched over with his face about six inches from the page in front of him. Though his workbook is closed, he is writing tiny numerals on a tight grid he has drawn with the ruler: "80, 85, 90, 110." There is no apparent connection between the unit instructions and the numbers he is writing. He continues in this manner, muttering and tracing out tiny numerals, for the rest of the class period. Five times during class, Marcus praises him without looking at the content of his work: "Good work, Chris."

In English, Demetrious, a particularly low-achieving student who has been having trouble following basic unit instructions, asks out loud, "What's a pronoun?" Cindy looks up from the papers on her desk and responds, "What does it say in the book? You have to read the book." This is followed by a minute or two of silence, after which Demetrious is distracted by another student distributing M&Ms from his jacket pocket. The classroom is quiet. At the end of the period, Cindy distributes small candies among the students, thanking them for "working so hard and being so good this whole week."

By virtually ignoring students who were working slowly or not working, and by rewarding students who showed at least minimal willingness to display a cooperative quiet in the classroom, Marcus and Cindy enabled students who wanted to complete their units to do so without the distraction of classroom arguments or confrontations. Both teachers maintained in this way generally peaceable environments where they themselves could do some grading or other paperwork, and both enjoyed a reputation among students for being "cool." In market terms, they sustained what might even be called a "good business climate": social rules were unspoken but mutually comprehended and usually respected by the teachers and the students, and thus the buying and selling of points and performances could proceed relatively unfettered.[2] In a typical class, one or two students would spend the time sleeping with their heads on a desk. Two or three would twist or braid their hair. A few would talk quietly among themselves but tend to their unit work at several-minute intervals. At least one, in most classes, would be determined to produce comparatively large quantities of looseleaf sheets and earn enough points for a Friday reward field trip or, ultimately, course credit. The majority of students scored 2 points for each category on their point cards on the majority of days.

Rick and Laura chose an alternate path. Determined to sustain what they regarded as a more school-like character than prevailed in English and math, they both refused to allow what was commonly referred to as "disrespect." "They [students] should not be allowed to get away with putting their heads down and being disrespectful of their instructors; this is a school," Laura said.

Both teachers engaged to this end in almost continuous skirmishes over the definition of the classroom, endlessly threatening students with a host of sanctions and eliciting in return frequent challenges and confrontations. Students cursed, kicked, spit, threw papers on the floor, carved graffiti into desktops, and walked out, slamming doors behind them. The teachers grew red-faced and raised their voices. Some days, there was so much arguing in the classrooms that it was virtually impossible even for the most diligent students to get any units finished. Following are typical exchanges.

Students in history are watching a video matched to a unit worksheet. One of the students, Darnell, lowers his head to the desk as the video begins. Immediately rushing over to stop the tape, Rick turns to the boy, glaring, and says: "This is not the time to sleep."

Darnell (pointing to worksheet): If I don't want to do it, I won't do it. I don't have to do it.

Rick: Wrong. You won't get credit if you don't do it. This is part of your assignment. You're being graded for how you cooperate on this assignment.

Darnell: I don't care, man. I won't do it.

Rick: You'll do it or you won't get any points for today for this class. (As he says this, he gathers the point cards spread over his desk and holds up the stack.)

Other students add their comments.

Joshua: This ain't even a real school, man. This is for discipline.

Rick: These credits are department of education credits. My job is to get you those credits.

Jasmine: You don't need those credits to get out of here.

Rick: I'm sorry you feel that way. That's the wrong attitude. I'm trying to help you get these credits. That's my job.

By this time, three students are making animal noises, grunting, snorting, and fidgeting in their seats. Darnell has his head on his desk, eyes closed.

Antwan (to Rick): You flagin' (that is, faking–as in "camouflaging"), man.

Rick turns on the video again, returns to his desk, and distributes zeroes in every category among the point cards.

* * * * *

Students have returned from lunch to their oceanography classroom. Hoping to stave off the usual post-lunch downturn in productivity, Laura stands at her desk and announces hurriedly: "Okay, now sit down, be quiet, get out your units." She distributes the folders, units, pencils, and looseleaf sheets. One boy asks to use the bathroom. Gesturing to the bulletin board, where a rules chart, excerpted from the student handbook and photocopied in large type, has been posted, Laura says: "First you need to tuck in your shirt, get out your work, and get on target." ("On target" is a phrase commonly used to describe a point-card score of two.)

Lonnie: I gotta go, man.

Laura: Get on target first.

Lonnie (standing and unzipping his pants): I said I gotta go.

Another student has brought a bag of potato chips back from the lunchroom; he drops a chip into the fish tank.

Laura: No one will go to the bathroom and no one will go on any field trips this week until everybody is on target and I see you doing your work. You know what you need to do.

Lonnie gets up and moves toward the bathroom.

Laura (in a loud voice): Sit down right now. You are not going anywhere until you are on target.

Lonnie: This school expects you to be sitting in your seat for eight hours. That's crazy shit. This ain't no boot camp, man. You can't do that.

Anika: That's right. You treat us like we're in boot camp sometimes. This is supposed to be a school. It's crazy. You need to relax. You can't make a big deal out of every little thing.

At this point, all seven students in the room indicate refusal to work: a few fold their arms, a few lean back in their chairs, and one places his head on the desk as if to take a nap. Laura's skin is bright red with aggravation. She sits quietly glaring for seven minutes. Then she says: "Okay, line up to go to the bathroom. We'll start over."

* * * * *

We are in Rick's class. Two girls sitting on desks are braiding a boy's hair. Their unit worksheets are on their desks; they tend to them briefly at intervals of three or four minutes.

Rick: Sit in your seats and stop doing that [braiding]. Michael is going to give a presentation. (This was one of Rick's special projects; the student was going to show the class a map of time zones and explain how to tell the time in California.)

Vanessa: I'm not stopping him.

Rick: Sit in your seat and listen and stop playing with Damon's hair.

Vanessa: I can hear from where I'm sitting. We can do this and that.

Rick (face turning red): Let me remind you that Promotion [hearing] is coming up and I'm doing your points right now.

Vanessa: I don't care. Fuck you. Go ahead and do my point card. I don't care. I'm giving you a one. One point for Rick.

The other students laugh vigorously; one laughs so hard that he falls out of his seat, knocking a stack of looseleaf sheets onto the floor, which subsequently have to be cleaned up as the rest of the class watches. Rick gives everyone zeroes on their point cards as the students continue to sit on the desks, and little attention is paid to any assignment for the rest of the period.

* * * * *

After several months of facing nearly continuous arguments in virtually every class, with his students earning very low point-card scores and not a single one securing any course credit, Rick imposed a new technique of behavior monitoring on top of the school's prevailing point system: whenever a student cursed or tried to walk out of the classroom, as happened frequently, Rick wrote down on paper a description of the episode, along with the time of day it happened. Several times daily he provided lists of such activities to the receptionist in the front office—in the left-hand column was the student's name, the curse word in quotation marks, and a brief account of any other infraction (e.g., "gave the finger"); in the right-hand column was the hour and class period. The receptionist rolled her eyes at these, and most of the staff quietly predicted, correctly as it turned out, that Rick would not last long on the job.

An entirely different system prevailed in boating, physical education, and the woodworking (vocational education) shop. These were regarded by students and some staff not as regular classes but rather, quite explicitly, as a kind of release from the type of work required by the other classes. It will be remembered that most of the woodworking equipment was broken or out of use due to materials or supplies shortages. Travis, however, made liberal use of the building's

large stock of hammers, drills, screwdrivers, and paintbrushes. Since he was required, in addition to teaching, to
maintain the school facilities and grounds, he engaged students in helping with the many odd jobs that always seemed
to be needed somewhere around the building. His class, to
which students were assigned for a week at a time, involved
a brief introductory lecture on shop rules, equipment, and
safety procedures, followed by a short written quiz to earn
class credit, all of which took up no more than a day or two.
The rest of the time was spent repainting old school furni-
ture; repairing broken pipes, tables, benches, and door-
knobs; or replacing lighting fixtures. Students would stand
around Travis as he demonstrated the steps involved in
replacing something like door-lock casings or hinges.
Depending on the job, students would usually get to paint or
drill or screw together something. Travis was usually standing nearby or alongside them, offering suggestions about the
position of the drills or the direction in which paintbrushes
needed to be moved.

At least twice during the week, usually three times, Travis
would take the students on a field trip to Lowe's or Home
Depot, the large national hardware store chains, sometimes
just for comparison shopping. On the way back, Travis
almost always stopped the van unofficially for an hour or so
at Burger King or Taco Bell. These side trips for fast food gen-
erated a great deal of enthusiasm among the students, but
they were somewhat clandestine; Travis neither noted all of
them in the school travel log nor requested reimbursement
or money from the petty cash fund. He either paid for the
food out of his own pocket or, just as often, let the students
pay their own way or treat one another if anyone had the
money. The students considered these activities "fun" and

certainly a relatively easy way to get school credit. Working on repair jobs, moreover, meant spending time in parts of the school building usually off limits to students, such as administrative offices, storage closets, and spaces underneath the lunchroom benches, which added a much appreciated element of novelty and transgression to the usual school routine.

Boating, the most popular class at school, was not regarded as a class at all. Kevin and Sean, for their part, called it a "reward for students who show us they can do well in their other classes." Writing the weekly schedule of class assignments, Kevin acted on his definition: misbehaving students sometimes got held back in history or oceanography even when boating loomed next on the regular cycle of classes. Dwayne, the boating teacher, conceived of his class as "a positive experience of something beautiful, a chance to experience nature," rather than as a route to high school credits or a reward for good behavior. Dwayne rarely insisted that students complete any of the unit worksheets or quizzes listed on the skills checklist form; consequently, few students ever earned formal credit for their participation. Rather, the course amounted to a week of mornings with a Red Cross workbook on water safety, followed by several hours of fishing or boating at lakes or beaches near the school. The group would eat lunch in the assembly hall about an hour early and then spend half an hour or so securing the canoes in the trailer, which was then hitched to a school van. Dwayne always turned on the van radio and, like Travis, usually sweetened the day by stopping at some local fast-food restaurant on the route back to school. Dwayne never forced anyone to board a canoe, and many first-time students, fearing the water, spent the first two days of the boating class cautiously watching the others from the safety of the shore. Dwayne would chuckle quietly and say, "Try it when you're ready," and eventually everyone was. The issue of point cards almost never came up. At least one student each week caught fish or crabs to bring home to his or her family, always a source of great excitement and commotion at the end of the school day when it came time to board the buses and everyone could see that one or two among them were carrying packages.

Physical education was similarly leisurely. Sherry modeled the class after the "workout" circuit of a professional gym, and there were field trips several times each week to private gymnasia, community centers, and university athletic centers in the city. Boys and girls good-naturedly competed with one another over who could lift the heaviest weights, marveling to watch their own muscles grow over the course of merely a week. Sherry prodded them gently–"Try another one, build those muscles a little"–and enlisted students in the job of "spotting" one another on the weightlifting machines. Physically occupied herself for most of each class period, Sherry almost never handled point cards or discussed their content with students during class time. Rather, she tended to wait until the very end of the period, just as students were lining up to leave, at that point hurriedly collecting the cards and filling them in (with "on target" scores, mostly) with neither confrontation nor ceremony.

Students never talked substantively among themselves about what they did in math, English or history. But they frequently discussed boating or the physical and vocational education classes ("Where did you go today with Mr. Travis?" or "Did you catch anything in Mr. Dwayne's?"), where there were no expectations of continuous unit production, the pace of work being determined instead by the nature of the task at hand: coats of paint needed to dry between applications; fish needed to be waited for; weights needed to be organized on the benches and bars. There was no rule of near-silence: hands-on work had a collective element that stressed informal group reflection and deliberation ("Your muscles getting big–you almost a real man now," was a joke heard among the boys in physical education, for example; in vocational education there were practical matters such as "Should we buy this size hinge or that one?"). The class value could be measured not exclusively in the officially approved terms of units completed and credits acquired but rather more purposefully in terms of direct intrinsic (and sometimes edible) rewards–muscles grown, fish caught, benches rebuilt, and so on. The purposefulness of work in these "hands-on" classes highlighted, paradoxically, the absence of intrinsic meaning in the academic curriculum. The definitional gulf separating leisurely classes from academic classes served to further reinforce within the school the prevailing cultural separation of work from leisure, of time spent working only for pay from time spent engaged in activities of intrinsic worth.

Accounting

Mirroring the school's prevailing market system of behavior management through the payment of predictable rewards and punishments, academic classroom relations took the form of a market economy, with looseleaf sheets its basic unit of calibration–a measure of the minimum quantity of compliant labor that students could exchange for points and course credit. Though there was little actual instruction, neither were there many displays of the kind of physically repressive supervisory authority that in the last two centuries has characterized juvenile justice programs–and some public schools, particularly in corporal-punishment states such as this one. Force emanated from the accounting of the teachers, with their stacks of point cards and file folders, and to a greater degree from the more abstract authority of the prevailing market in merit, with its predictable calculus of so many credits for so many completed units, so many points and days off for so much apparent productive output and display of commitment.

With its rewards for productivity and its consequences for recalcitrance, academic education at Academy was a workplace-like negotiation between student sellers of educational and behavioral labor (underlined nouns, filled-in worksheet blanks, silence in class) and teacher buyers designated to pay, evenhandedly and according to the objective rule of predictable institutional laws, the symbolic wages of points, class credit, and leisure time (field trips, "rec"). Work was differentiated from play in the division of classes: play was collective, enjoyable, intrinsically valuable; work was dull, individualized, and lacking in intrinsic meaning, done exclusively for the sake of the symbolic payments available in exchange. Students derived what seemed remarkably sparse substantive content from their units in history, English, math or oceanography; they got little of the kind of vocational training that might have equipped them to secure durable jobs in the local economy. What they practiced, however, was sustained engagement with a market system.

Popular conceptions of juvenile delinquency–conceptions underpinning recent "tough-on-crime" policy efforts aimed at removing "troubled" children from mainstream public school classrooms–hold that delinquents are incorrigible troublemakers, pathologically lacking in self-control and the ability to discriminate; rule-breaking is regarded as an innate feature of their personalities, school failure virtually an inevitability. But rule-breaking at Academy was not spread evenly across classes and settings. Academy students could be calm sometimes and "wild" at others; those performing acceptably in one class could wind up assigned to a work crew during another. Perennial troublemakers chose certain moments to comply with school rules; conversely, usually cooperative students could at times make some teachers miserable. But as will be seen in the next chapter, there were logical patterns to student refusal.

5

Student Reaction to
the Market System

ACADEMY STUDENTS were not so far out of the mainstream that they embraced enthusiastically and naively the stultifying academic curriculum offered to them. On the contrary, student life at the school was characterized by considerable resistance to the rationalization embodied in the unit system, as well as a great deal of sarcasm and refusal in the face of picayune rules of behavior management.

The daily behavioral rules at Academy tended to strip students of what sociologist Erving Goffman (1961) has called "the usual ritual supplies"—food, cigarettes, certain clothing, jewelry, music, and specialized language—out of which the members of an institution can build identities and work out the status rankings of their group. In place of these traditional commodities, students had to seek other raw materials by which to distinguish themselves and demonstrate their allegiances.[1] The school attempted to provide such materials in the form of ranks, points, and school credit, the market in merit with its associated array of privileges and rewards. Students had to participate in this adult-sanctioned social economy—submitting their looseleaf sheets and displaying compliance with school behavioral rules in classes and assemblies—if they were to complete the school program and win their release. But every market has its tensions and imperfections. Like producers in the workplace outside the school, who face the daily prospect of mechanical and repetitive labor with little intrinsic reward, students sometimes complied with and sometimes resisted the call to work. They sometimes embraced and sometimes ignored the payoffs available to the most productive, striving at certain times, within certain limits, and with varying outcomes, to claim some measure of autonomy from the terms the school offered them.[2] To this end, they alternated compliance with refusal. Work slowdowns, ironic commentary, teasing, and foot dragging—a variety of little acts of sabotage and sometimes outright defiance—were the bane of the teacher and the school manager.[3]

Flagin'

In academic classrooms, the primary sabotage was to show effort without actually exerting much of it. Students referred to this as "flagin'"—as in "camouflaging." As one sang to another in rap form, jokingly, in English class one morning: "You show that you know; but you don't know; but you can go." It was not unusual, for example, for students laboriously to write, erase, and rewrite several times their names, the date, or the unit number at the top of their looseleaf sheets, which could take up ten minutes or more of a class period. Some students spent fifteen minutes or more carefully writing numerals in a column along the left-hand margins of their sheets, numbering the questions in an assignment or unit before starting any substantive work on them. If the assignment involved vocabulary words, students sometimes would write out all the words first–as many as twenty-five in some cases–leaving a space between them of one or two lines to be filled in later in the period or some other time, if ever. Most common was for students to copy in detail all the questions and instructions in a unit, leaving spaces for answers or responses, before actually starting–or never actually starting–any of the unit work. This could easily take up an entire class period. Seventeen-year-old Albert managed one day to spread a very brief English unit assignment across three looseleaf sheets. On the first sheet he wrote his name, the date, and the unit number. On the second sheet he wrote his name, the date, and one-word answers to the first two questions in the unit: "What do you call a sentence that ends in a period?" (correct answer, copied from the workbook: "a statement") and "What do you call a sentence that ends in a question mark?" (correct answer, copied from the workbook: "a question"). On the third sheet he copied eight brief sentences from the workbook, adding the appropriate period or question mark at the end of each. Then he asked Cindy for a stapler and took up a span of several minutes aligning the corners of his three papers before stapling them together. With these labors he managed to fill an hour's class period, at the end of which Cindy noted with a nod, "You working today."

Students frequently walked over to the wastepaper basket to throw out looseleaf sheets, which they would crumple thoroughly, and sometimes remarkably slowly, into tight little balls. It was not uncommon for some students to make three or four such trips during a class period. There was frequent pencil sharpening. Students routinely took the last twenty minutes of class to read and reread their point cards, inspect their file folders, rearrange the filed-away looseleaf sheets, staple loose pages, or erase a variety of stray pencil marks. Some asked teachers for Promotion Request Forms, signally officially their allegiance to school processes, and used class time to fill out these forms as slowly as possible. Others asked, "Can I see my point card?" and spent inordinate lengths of time reading and rereading their scores. Those unable merely to sit sometimes took time to decorate their folders with elaborate pencil drawings, usually of cars, guns, marijuana leaves, or gang names in the case of the boys or, among the girls, the names or nicknames of boyfriends. A few quoted from popular rap songs: the words "Thug Life," for instance, appeared on one boy's file folder, a reference to rap artist Tupac Shakur (who was shot to death the following year).

Among students tending to the content of their unit assignments, few sought 100-percent-correct unit papers; on the contrary, when encountering a question they couldn't answer, most simply skipped it and moved on. Some announced outright their refusal to work in one particular class or another: "I won't do no work for no white man," one boy said; his teacher sent him into a "consequence" work crew. Others made a point of minimizing their efforts: "Do exactly what it says in the instructions," one top-ranking student told a new entrant on his first day in English. "Don't do any more than you need to. Just answer the questions on this unit. Don't do anything except what it says you have to do, or you'll be wasting your time." A few students "borrowed" papers to copy from their friends, passing them quickly back and forth, sometimes in exchange for cigarettes or candy, which would be distributed either surreptitiously in class, passed from palm to palm under the desktops, or more likely between classes or at the start of lunch or assembly periods. Some quietly arranged to work in tandem, one doing even-numbered questions, for example, another doing the odds, and then exchanging papers when the teacher was not looking.

Sometimes students would attempt to initiate group discussion about some topic they knew to be of interest to the staff and therefore an acceptable use of classroom time. A student would initiate a complaint, for example, about some other teacher in the school: "I hate Miss Laura. She's crazy"; "He's too strict"; "He never listens"; "We just sit around in that class"; "Nobody knows how to do math around here; these teachers are useless." Complaints could take up half a class period or more. Committed to a school program model that cast them in the role of advisors and mentors, rather than mere work supervisors, teachers usually tolerated these conversations, intervening only minimally when voices were raised loud enough to be heard outside the room. Moreover, these conversations were one of the only sources of information about other teachers' specific classroom management styles and goings-on in other classes. In any case, they were a means by which students could avoid classwork without getting into trouble over it.

Both in class and outside it, students flouted behavioral rules, often just to the point of taunting their teachers but not enough to incur onerous disciplinary sanctions. A few students routinely challenged the official ban on jewelry, for example, by wearing religious icons, which staff hesitated to discourage. One boy came to school wearing an enormous gold cross on a necklace, for example; staff did not make him remove it, though jewelry was forbidden. Each day several students brought hats to school, sometimes draping them over their heads like towels or rags, thereby challenging but not quite breaking outright the school ban on hat wearing. There

were girls who almost daily wore short mini-skirts and reveal-
ing shirts, explicitly banned by the school rule book. They
narrowly circumvented the discipline of the staff, however,
by bringing overshirts to cover the revealed skin. "You know
you can't wear that," Cindy told Terry one day after she'd come
to school in a tight half-top exposing both cleavage and navel.
"I know," Terry said in matter-of-fact tones. "I brought a shirt
for it." Students deliberately answered staff questions in overly
quiet tones, having then to repeat themselves; they walked
from class to class far too slowly, having then to be told to
speed up; they pretended not to hear what was said to them,
having then to get it repeated; they saw and then deliberately
ignored the scraps of paper and bits of food that stuck between
the benches in the assembly hall after lunch, which meant
staff would have to spend time supervising recleaning work
or doing the cleaning themselves.

Students were not allowed to talk openly about curfew
violations or other illegal activities; teachers thwarted such
talk with calls to "quiet down," particularly in homeroom.
But adventures outside school were a source of excitement
and status, and students found means legitimately to report
them. Every so often students brought in pocket-sized photo
albums depicting late-night parties and alcohol consump-
tion; they passed these among the benches during breakfast
or when morning assembly was starting. One boy came to
school wearing a large and obviously home-made bandage
on his wrist. Staff and students asked him about it several
times during the day, each time granting him license to
relate a lengthy and titillating story about having cut himself while jumping a fence in flight from pursuing sheriff's
deputies. A girl cut her buttocks running from police; for
two weeks she was exempted from having to sit up on her

stitches, and students spent the first few minutes of every class period discussing the matter of her possible scarring ("What white skin look like with scars?" "Did the police point a gun at you?"). A few students came to school with purple bite marks on their necks, a quiet but powerful symbolic announcement of out-of-school romantic liaisons. For girls, of course, pregnancy was the ultimate advertisement of having evaded the curfew monitor.

Some students made a kind of game out of marshalling officially sanctioned language and symbolism on behalf of agendas other than those of the school. Here is a typical example.

It is a hot afternoon; the students are visibly uncomfortable. A fistfight breaks out in oceanography. Three students in the English class, which is meeting right next door this week to accommodate repairs in the south wing hallway, want to watch the events unfold. As they ignore their teacher's warnings and crowd into the doorway between the two classrooms, Ed appears on the scene to block their way. "You don't belong here," he says in a loud voice.

Tramont (calling to Laura in the oceanography classroom): Hey, do you have my point card? I'm looking for my point card.

Jerome (to Ed): I think I left my point card in here. Rec day is coming up.

Franklin (to Laura): Did you mark my point card yet?

Deferring to the apparent show of interest in matters of school policy, Ed moves aside, and Laura switches attention from her own students to those in the doorway, promising to have point cards ready by the end of the period. The fistfight stops momentarily; the fighters break for a moment, smiling broadly as they relish the deception their onlookers are achieving. The students who were able to catch a brief view of the proceedings now return, smirking, to their own classroom, where they report on the fight's participants.

Students often engaged in an exaggerated compliance with school rules, creating a drama of ironic obedience. One day a boy with a widely talked-about history of drug dealing, for example, announced with deadpan tone of voice as a morning-assembly "Safety Tip" that students should "Just say no to drugs." This inspired paroxysms of laughter among the other students at their benches and prompted another adjudicated former drug dealer–who according to school gossip had been selling drugs from his mother's house after school–to raise his hand and announce when selected: "If you have to concentrate, don't smoke." Staff quieted the commotion ("Settle down or we'll start [assembly] over") but left the announcements themselves without comment.

Morning assembly was the preferred forum for these performances of tongue-in-cheek compliance. It was not unusual, for example, for more than two students in a row to raise their hands and volunteer the very same safety tip. "Buckle up," followed by the requisite applause, would be followed by another "Buckle up," and more requisite applause, and then there would be a "Don't drink and drive," followed by applause, followed again by a "Friends don't let friends drive drunk," followed by applause.

Some students were well-known in the school for their imaginative humor: seventeen-year-old LeVon was constantly annoying his teachers with his almost continuous, barely audible under-the-breath mutterings. Regarded by students and staff alike as a "good student"–he could finish class assignments with ease when he wanted to and almost always disengaged himself, retreating to his dittoes and workbooks, when fistfights or arguments flared among the other students–he could at times display biting sarcasm and inspire rollicking laughter. When a young social worker visited Academy as part of her orientation to the juvenile justice system, with which she had just taken a job, LeVon stood in the oceanography classroom, his dreadlocks framing a broad, toothy smile, and welcomed her with a firm handshake and his "whitest" tone of voice, exaggerating the vowels and consonants: "Pleeeezed to meeeet you, Ma'am. Welcome to oceanahhhhhh-graphy. Would you like to see some of our books and payyyy-pers?" As soon as the duly impressed visitor was out of the room, LeVon turned abruptly on his heels, faced the teacher, and asked, sneering, in a gruff voice: "How many points do I get?" Even Laura, who indeed granted bonus points, couldn't help but join the students in their laughter. LeVon had not only complied with school rules; he had displayed a smug mastery over them.

Matt, a cheerful, easy-going seventeen-year-old, graduated from Academy in record time, five months, by volunteering for every assembly and working diligently in almost every class. All the staff held him up as an example to the others; he "made rec" almost every other Friday; his attendance was nearly perfect. But when teachers weren't listening, Matt would tell his peers in no uncertain terms that he was "using" the school as much as accepting its prescriptions. "I'm getting outta here because I know how to work the system," he told a new student one morning whom he had known previously from public school.

What you have to do is what they want to see you do. You say what you know they want you to say. You be positive–you say, `I'm feeling great. I'm doing great. Nice to meet you.' That's what you have to do. A lot of people in here don't do that–they don't give 'em what they want. But I know how to get out of here. I'm moving up fast in rank because I'll do what it takes. . . . I'm playing the game, giving them what they want to see.

Sometimes in assemblies he would offer, along with his usual "Positive Thought" or "Safety Tip" for the day, his own countdown to release. "I'll be out in three months, just watch," he would announce, to laughter and robust applause from the group. In this way he displayed overt compliance with the program–earning for his meritorious performances high points and a coveted early release–but maintained a posture of loyalty exclusively to his own ostensibly loftier goals.

Rick showed a video in class one day depicting state historic landmarks. At one point, at the sight of gleaming downtown skyscrapers, one of the students announced gleefully (and falsely), "Hey, Joe, that's the bank we robbed." The other students tumbled out of their chairs with laughter as Rick demanded silence. On one of Travis's unofficial field trips to Burger King, in line just ahead of the group at the cash register was a man one student recognized as the attorney who had prosecuted him. Situating himself barely inches from the man's ear, the student whispered, "You put me here. Now lend me some money so I can get some food." Pale and somewhat shaken, the attorney took his bag from the woman running the cash register and left without comment as the students, all grinning with triumph, watched him.

One morning a powerful state legislator visited the school. She was a few minutes early, the school buses a few minutes late. Instead of starting the normally scheduled routine, school administrators made the unusual decision to cancel homeroom and morning assembly, sending the students straight from the buses to their first-period classes. The intent was to have them in class for the visit, since the legislator was regarded as a strong child advocate and supporter of education. Teachers quickly distributed folders and units; the students settled to work quietly at their desks. Ed made rounds in the building, poking his head briefly into each class to remind everyone to "act appropriately." The boys tucked their shirt-tails into their pants and stored their hats under the desks; the girls removed their earrings and stopped chewing their gum. Everyone arranged their loose-leaf sheets in neat stacks, sat up straight, and positioned their pencils in their hands. The legislator was ushered to the south wing to observe English, math, and then history. The students stood somberly, lining up to shake her hand and then return quietly to their seats. "Welcome to our school," they repeated one after another with each handshake. As soon as the legislator was out of the building, staff collected point cards and graded them generously. Then, at lunch, Ed stood at the front of the assembly hall and praised the group: "We are really showing what this school is about." But the students, who had played along perfectly, couldn't resist the chance for a laugh. "You teachin' us to kiss ass," one said from the front bench, generating giggles from the students around him. "Know what you learn in this program?" said another to a teacher standing within earshot. "You learn to suck up." Staff ignored both the comments and the snickering accompanying them.

Students made more overt and direct claims of autonomy. "It's my body; let me do what I want with it," was a common refrain among the boys, who were asked virtually hourly to tuck their shirt-tails in their pants. "Why you care about my jewelry?" a few complained when called upon to remove earrings or necklaces. "You getting you some business. Get you some business somewhere else," a girl told any teacher who asked about her earrings and clothing, though she knew eventually she'd have to remove them. Night curfews were considered a particularly distasteful affront to bodily self-governance, and students complained about them frequently. "I got things to do, man," was the insistent cry from boys reminded to be home by the curfew hour. Sometimes, more humorously, students accused staff of moral and legal violations. "You on drugs," some would say, particularly to Laura and Rick. "You got any dank [marijuana]?" "Is that car stolen?" "He's flagin," said one student to a staff member after Sean, the executive director, stopped to shake her hand while making his rounds through the building. "He be smiling all the time, acting like everything's good. He's so fake. I hate that."

The Ramifications of Refusal

There were limits to what students could "get away with," as staff put it, in refusing to give themselves wholeheartedly to what the school requested of them. Students paid, sometimes dearly, for their more dramatic acts of defiance. Cedric, for example, mustering remarkable self-discipline, refused for several months to talk even briefly with Rick, his advisor, though he conversed easily and good-naturedly with the other teachers. Rick kept him after school to try to get him to do his schoolwork. He held him back in history class when the rest of the students in his group had moved on. He drove him home instead of letting him ride the school van and then parked in front of the wrong house just to elicit a response. Still no reaction. Rick put him on a work crew for a few days. He tried apologizing for wrongs he might have committed. Still nothing. "I'm not going to talk to him," Cedric told Cindy when she asked what he was doing. "I hate him." Perhaps not surprisingly, Rick considered the display to be further evidence of the very pathologies that had brought Cedric to Academy in the first place ("He is in bigger trouble than I thought."). The result for Cedric, ultimately, was months added to his tenure at the school.

Refusals could have legal ramifications. Jamil, nearing his eighteenth birthday, was too old, in practical terms, ever to return to public high school. A shy, sensitive person given to bouts of brooding silence and occasional bursts of anger, he complained for months—as did many students, though none more insistently than Jamil—that he needed a GED preparation class instead of the standard high school credits available through the Academy program. Rather than acknowledging his claims, with which they generally concurred, or even granting their rationality, the teachers attempted to keep him focused instead on the point system and its requirements. "You have to show us you can graduate here first," Kevin, the education director, told him many times. "Keep working on your units." Frustrated beyond limit, Jamil eventually stopped coming to school—"absconding," as staff put it—the ultimate declaration of independence. "I couldn't take that place," he said later.

I hated it. They just be messing with you, trying to make you do all that work so you never know when you getting out, when you graduating. . . . I just had to get outta there. I don't want to go back to school. I need to get my GED, that's what I need. I been talking to some guys thirty-five, thirty years old. They say the thing they most sorry about is they never got their GED.

Because of his legal status, leaving the school meant breaking a court order; wanted by police, Jamil went into hiding, according to staff discussions.

Fighting was against the rules and everybody knew it; sometimes, however, students would not relent. When they perceived school discipline to have failed, or to have delivered unacceptable outcomes, they meted out their own forbidden and often frightening brand of justice. Some days, staff had to work hard to keep them safe from each other and from the legal ramifications of the disciplinary system some of them imposed on one another.

One boy from a comparatively well-off family had a new, professionally done hairstyle every few days. In his jacket pockets he often brought tape cassettes or candy, and when asked to share, he sometimes made the other students take on the ritualized gestures of deference prevalent among street gangs. They had to say "Please, may I," for example, and hold out their hands to him with the palms facing down. Staff discussed his case briefly at a meeting one afternoon. "He teasin' them," said Cindy. "He a `pretty boy.' I don't think they're gonna take it if he keep doing it." Cindy's predictions were correct. One morning soon afterward, a student snatched a tape cassette out of the boy's jacket pocket as two others asked him for candy. When he told them, "You ain't

man enough to take this [candy] from me," one of the boys
hit him and pinned him to the ground while the other,
Keshawn, grabbed the candy and ate it. The boy screamed
that he was being robbed; he wanted to press charges. Staff
broke up the fight and called the police, who arrested
Keshawn, took him to the regional juvenile detention center, and eventually, it was said, charged him with a felony
(strong-arm robbery) that likely would change forever his
"face sheet" (list of legal charges). Keshawn had attained top
rank and was scheduled to graduate in a matter of weeks;
the ceremony was promptly cancelled. The student who'd
done the hitting, meanwhile, ran from the building, disappeared, and was subsequently "wanted" by police. The following morning, in an effort to confiscate weapons and prevent retaliatory attacks among the students, staff organized
a search. The stolen tape cassette was found in a jacket
pocket during frisking. Staff decided they'd been too lax
about searches and vowed, at their afternoon meeting, to
clamp down on illicit candy and other forbidden objects.

Other times there were tense moments:

Seven students are in oceanography. Jose, a quiet boy,
has become a target for taunts from the other students
in the school. A black student, Jordan, leans over to the
desk. "Que pasa, Muchacho?" he taunts. There is no
response. Jordan tries again. Again, no response. The
exchange is repeated five times until finally Jose turns
to him and screams: "I'll kick your fucking ass, man.
I'm tired of you." Commentary starts among some white
students in another corner of the room.

Allison: Ooh, that quiet boy got a mouth.

Johnny (licking his lips in the direction of Allison):
Mmmm.

Allison (to Johnny): You ugly dog. Don't be checking
out people who ain't checking you out back.

Johnny: Whore. Bitch. (Then, to Jose) Muchacho.

The teacher notices Ed, the assistant director, walking outside the classroom. She calls him in. He tells the
class, "If you don't do your work, there is a staff person
who will stay after school and work with you while you
do it." The students quiet down briefly.

Johnny, whom some of his peers call "country boy,"
is wearing high-heeled cowboy boots and a polished
leather belt with a large brass buckle. His hair is dyed
bright blond, almost yellow, and on his t-shirt is a list:
"Ten reasons why a horse is mo' better than a woman":

> You can ride a horse any time you want! You don't
> have to hold her when you're done riding her!
> Hay is cheaper than roses!
> Have you ever heard a horse bitch?
> A horse comes when you whistle!
> Shoes don't cost as much!
> When a horse is too old to ride, you can still make
> glue!
> You can sell the ol' nag and buy a new filly!
> A horse is happy when you ride another horse!
> The harder you spur, the harder they buck!

After a few quiet minutes, Johnny starts talking about
fishing for eels and finding hallucinogenic mushrooms
at the lake near his house (a variety of these mushrooms is ubiquitous in the region, growing on ferment-

ing piles of cow or horse manure and boiled for a "tea" popular among the rural students).

Johnny: I found some bad mushrooms yesterday, man. (Then, to Allison) You suck Billy's cock?

Allison: No, asshole.

Shantil: You sucked Billy's cock.

Laura (red-faced, to group): Let me remind you that I have your point cards here and there are expectations that you show appropriate attitudes and behavior. Ed is outside right now.

Johnny: I ain't doing this [unit work].

Matthew: Just shut up, man, just stop talking.

Johnny: Fuck you.

Allison: Don't you know the meaning of 'shut your mouth'?

Matthew: Listen to him; he keep running his mouth. There something wrong with you, man.

Laura at this point demands that they all turn their desks to face the nearest wall, with no student facing another.

Shantil (tapping a pencil on his desk, singing): You ain't got the money, doo doo doo . . .

Johnny: I hate that rap shit, man.

Shantil (sardonically, imitating Johnny's voice): I don't hate black people. I just hate that rap music.

The three black students in the class start laughing hard. Laura rushes out to retrieve Ed once again, telling him, "There are some racial problems between the kids."

Johnny: That's it. I'm tired of this. (Clenching his fist, he walks to the desk where Shantil is sitting.)

Jose and Matthew get up quickly and flank the desk, glaring. A fight is about to begin.

Laura runs back into the room and, coming up behind him, taps Johnny on the shoulder. "Let's go," she says. He refuses to move. She grips him hard. "Let's go now. Everything is under control. We're going outside." She then tells the other students to sit down. She and Johnny stand talking just outside the classroom door; Laura keeps her hand on the doorknob. By the time they re-enter the room, the period is almost over. The students return their folders to Laura's desk and move toward the door. Johnny, standing in the doorway, suddenly yells: "Those fucking niggers. I hate them so much." Laura leads the group, now very quiet, to the assembly hall for lunch.

At the afternoon staff meeting, Laura notes that the situation has grown more urgent. There is a tension in the building. The black students have been conspicuously silent all through lunch and into the afternoon; quiet nods and glances have been exchanged among them. The teachers are alarmed. "We have to do something about the racial slurs," Laura says. "We are seeing a lot of this right now." The other staff agree. Ed says he will handle it.

The next morning at the start of assembly, Ed announces to the students: "There is something important we need to talk about. We are hearing a lot of racial language here lately. That is inappropriate. I will not tolerate it. No 'cracker,' no 'white boy,' no 'nigger,' no 'Hispanic,' no nothing like that. I am serious. Anybody here likes or dislikes somebody based on the color of their skin, I pray for you. That is not the kind of people we want to be. I judge people by the content of their character, by their attitude, by the way they carry themself. Not by their race, not by their color. We're gonna show respect in here today. If I hear one racial remark, you will hear from me."

Everyone is dismissed to first period. Johnny goes to math. A teacher had called in sick that day, so the students are doubled up in some of the classes. Math is crowded, with every seat filled. One student sits at Marcus's desk; Marcus stands in the doorway. The day is very hot and humid, a Southern kind of heat, and the classroom is stuffy.

Within seconds, five black students huddle in a circle around Johnny. There is a thud as someone hits him. Johnny's snarling can be heard from inside the huddle. Marcus rushes to the center of it, pushes his body inside the circle of boys, wraps Johnny in his arms, and drags him out to the hall. Marcus calls to Cindy next door: "Get supervision." Sherry, assigned to supervise the "consequences" work crew that morning, appears at the door and quietly gathers the five black students, leading them to the assembly hall, where she commands them to sit. Marcus escorts Johnny, who is sweating profusely, trembling, and cursing in a rage, to the front office. The students do not reveal to Sherry who actually threw the punch. She puts all of them on a work crew for the rest of the week.

All the teachers watched Johnny closely the rest of the week to make sure he was not attacked again. Several times

Ed and Sean held private conferences with him in their offices; there was a call to his mother, who "cussed like a drunken sailor," as Ed reported it at the afternoon meeting. But more than once again during the week, Johnny told other students they were "niggers" and "monkeys," and throughout the building there were murmurs about revenge. The staff deliberated what to do, worrying that someone eventually was going to bring a weapon into the school. "We can't keep him safe if he keeps that up," Laura said. "I hate to say it, but he's digging his own hole," Marcus said.

Within two weeks, Sean had Johnny transferred by the juvenile justice counselor to a higher-end treatment program. One of the five boys who had attacked him was arrested not long afterward on an unrelated charge of attempted murder. Jose, the Hispanic youth the other students taunted, soon absconded from the school and was not seen again, though his advisor believed his parents knew where he was hiding.

There were other tense situations as students meted out their own justice, and following which there would be consequences within the market system of merit.

The students file into the assembly hall. Rick's class arrives a few minutes before the others. It is a hot and very uncomfortable humid day; the students are particularly restless and frustrated. One of the younger boys, Billy, who has been a discipline problem for all the staff, grabs some of the other students' hats and runs off with them. The older boys chase him around the room, weaving in and out of the rows of benches, trying to get their hats back. As the boys near him, Billy clamps onto them with outstretched arms, trying, mostly unsuccessfully, to fling them down to the ground. It is obvious that the older boys are increasingly aggravated with this taunting; they are cursing, spitting.

Billy grabs James, a muscular boy with gold teeth who has "come down" from one of the higher-level programs for violent youth. James shoves him off with an elbow. But Billy comes again. More pushing. Then again. Soon the two boys are entangled on the floor, rolling over one another, with James throwing his fist into Billy's sides. Suddenly there is a turn of events. James bites Billy's neck, hard, grasping with his mouth as the two roll over and over. He shoves his tongue into Billy's ear. Billy starts shrieking: "He's licking me! He's licking me!" Now Billy is panicking, struggling to push away. James pounds Billy's ear with his tongue, and Billy shrieks, "Get off me! Get off me!" Rick moves toward them, yelling, "Stop it."

James suddenly loosens his grip. Billy scrambles up, cursing. "He fuckin' licked me, man." Drips of sweat are rolling down the sides of his face; he wipes his cheeks with his hands as the other students jeer and curse. "Fuck you, man." But the students are eyeing James with some suspicion now as they move toward their seats on the benches. Rick shakes his head in disgust as the other classes begin filing in for lunch. There will be zeroes on the point cards and notations in the behavior reports.

Acting Rationally in the Market System

Subject to ongoing monitoring and evaluation, tethered to the rank-and-point economy of punishments and rewards, conversation and gesture at Academy could not be characterized as the "ideal speech situation," as Jurgen Habermas (1984, 1987) might call it, of open and uncoerced truth-seeking dialogue and communication. Academy did not live up to the ideal of "raw, unadulterated affection" promised in school promotional brochures. Nor was it the "apprenticeship of responsibility" that criminologist Edgardo Rotman (1994) imagines as the true core of rehabilitation. On the other hand, speech and gesture at Academy were not the dominated communication of the prison, with its deference born of fear and its discipline the threat of harsh physical deprivation. Rather, student action was performative and instrumental—its gestures were those of the marketplace. Successful students learned to measure and temper their communications, keeping them within permissible boundaries and exchanging them for points, credits, and early release, the symbolic wages of the meritocracy. Students embraced, essentially, the technical-rational orientation to language and performance that characterizes formal economic transactions, the rationality and deliberation of calculated self-interest. Behavior was currency; each speech act, an exchange token.

Nevertheless, students engaged in a kind of indigenous slapstick, reserving means and moments for illicit laughter at the institution's expense. They dragged their feet, faked their work, pushed rules to their limits, and poked fun at their teachers. At times they made a mockery of their own compliance. Flagin' and joking were means by which students could in some sense disavow the pervasive instrumentalization of action, even while training themselves to its rhythms. Yet sometimes defiance was self-defeating and injurious, beyond the limits of what teachers would tolerate; at times it was convulsive.

Workplaces bestow their rewards on workers with a certain instrumental style of self-conduct, on those with an intent to buy and sell and an appropriate level of desire for the available payments. They punish those, on the other hand, who are overly aggressive or not aggressive enough, overly ambitious or not ambitious enough. Such is the social economy from which Academy emerges and to which students, like workers in the formal economy, had ultimately to accommodate. As one school manager said, "We've all learned to act the way we need to act in different situations. We act one way with our grandmothers and another way with our boss. They [students] can learn that too. They'll need to learn it if they're going to succeed out there."

6

Teachers and the Market System

STUDENTS' OBSTINACY, sarcasm, and outright defiance posed for teachers two nagging quandaries. First, like business managers in the formal economy who find themselves charged with administering the labor of recalcitrant employees, teachers unable to elicit from students consistent or conscientious performance became subject at times to the scrutiny of their own productivity-conscious supervisors. The worth of a point, in terms of the kinds of student performances teachers should demand, was an almost daily topic of conversation; the managerial proficiency of individual teachers—measured as the degree to which they could sustain the desired exchange rate—was a subject of continual interest to everyone on the staff. Teachers could be disciplined for not performing. Yet clamping down on students, as some teachers found, was no sure way to generate the sought-after results.

Their second quandary was that Academy teachers had the job of translating broad institutional aims, derived from juvenile justice and education, into the practical language of ranks, points, and school credit and, conversely, of translating the ground-level vocabulary of points and ranks into higher-level claims about program effectiveness. A kind of logical operation was called for that connected the theory of the justice system to the measurement instrument of points.[1] When student performances reached not quite the desired level of earnestness, however, when flagin' (camouflaging, or faking) replaced effort and compliance was accompanied by irony and exaggeration, it became difficult to claim with certainty that education or rehabilitation of some kind had actually been achieved, even when points had been acquired. Seeking the high-minded but operationally elusive goal of "turning kids' lives around," as they called it, teachers faced a degree of uncertainty as to the meaning and measure of success on the job. "Make sure you are not rewarding conformity for its own sake," as Sean said, pointing to the heart of the dilemma inherited from the days of the Elmira penitentiary. "Remember that we are seeking deeper, long-lasting behavioral change."

In this context, teachers, like their students, found their own ways to mitigate the rigidities and paradoxes of the prevailing market system and to some degree bend the school to their own interests, intentions, and orientations.[2] They made certain adjustments to the point system, withheld information from others, made exceptions in doling out rewards and consequences, distanced themselves from certain problems and policies, and initiated classroom practices, sometimes disapproved by the higher ranks, that rendered their daily exertions personally valuable, meaningful, and significant. These efforts constituted the core of what staff regarded as their primary task: "Working with the kids."

Under Scrutiny

Daily admonitions from Sean or Ed–"You should've put him on [a work crew]," for instance, or "You should've tried counseling him"–reminded teachers continuously of being under the watchful eyes of their near-at-hand supervisors. The message hit home some times more strongly than others. It was felt particularly keenly during an exchange one morning in the conference room, where staff had gathered for a monthly staff meeting and workshop. The teachers were somewhat uneasy. A newcomer in line for a management job, it was said, was observing the school for a period of a few weeks. Over the previous days, he had not only observed but offered criticisms as well, particularly of what he regarded as overly lax discipline. A few teachers felt he had intruded.

Ed opened the meeting by suggesting there had been some "point card inflation." The previous week, he said, "we had one kid over 400 [points] for the week, several over 380. That is escalation. I love all our kids, but I don't see our students performing to that level." There were nods around the table. In a kind of pedagogical tone, as if initiating some kind of recitation among the staff, he asked: "When does a student get a 15 [for the day]?"

Travis: Never.

Rick: When others are being very disruptive and fighting and that student deliberately stays out of it and keeps doing his work. That happens about every two months.

Dwayne: The only time I've given it is when a kid actually did CPR on a victim while we were out with the boats.

John (a replacement physical education teacher who stayed only a few months on the job): I can see what Rick is saying: we have to reward the kids, too.

Travis: But not fighting is just meeting expectations, maybe a 12.

Newcomer: We should not be inflating the points. If you give a kid a 15, the next day he's gonna act out because he knows he's got the points. Or sometimes he act out today because he knows tomorrow he can get a 15 so he don't have to worry about it today. You got to see how a kid is acting overall.

Carol (one of the community liaisons): But we got to judge a kid today, not last week. We go with what we're seeing today.

Newcomer: But you don't forget about last week.

Rick: What happens when a kid does his work, but then cusses you out in the last fifteen minutes of the class?

Newcomer: He gets a one, because he did something.

Rick: No, he gets a zero. When a student says "fuck you" and walks out of supervision every single day, I give him zeroes every single day. And nothing changes.

Newcomer: You are not doing all you can for the kid. . . . If staff give consistent zeroes, that staff is not using good counseling skills. . . . You got to use your skills and maybe call Ed and not let that happen. What else can you do with the kid?

Rick: Well, I have a box over here that I'm supposed to use, and I've pulled everything out of it. Now you're

saying because I've run out of things to do that we
should send him to jail.

Newcomer: No. I'm saying there are things you can do.
Get a meeting, bring in juvenile justice, the counselor.

Sean walks in. All eyes are now on him.

Sean: The point system is the basic premise of your
empowerment in the classroom; it's the basic tool to
change the behavior in the school. I used to want to get
the points completely standardized with everybody
doing exactly the same thing. Now I know that's impossible; you can't get it. But we need to come closer to that.

Rick was embarrassed by the attention visited upon him,
and the other teachers were sympathetic. Discussion of individual staff members' classroom management problems
rarely took place during formal meetings involving the entire
staff. Later, when some of the teachers went out for lunch,
Kevin poked Rick in the ribs and teased him about the visitor's scrutiny. "You're not doing all you can. . . . You got to use
your skills. What's the matter with you, man?" Everyone
laughed heartily.

Like managers in the world of work who know they are
under scrutiny, staff attempted at times to clamp down on
recalcitrant producers and enforce the generalized building-
wide rate of point-and-rank exchange to which Sean was
ever aspiring. Their efforts, however, were virtually always
thwarted. When a few teachers decided to make the work
crews "harder," for example, by assigning students for several hours to dig and then fill a deep trench in the vacant lot
adjacent to the south wing of the building, Sean warned them,
angrily, that "meaningless work gives the wrong message; we
are not a boot camp." When Laura suggested at a meeting that

misbehaving students be made to clean bathrooms, Sean insisted that such practices are "not in keeping with the philosophy of the program." When several teachers wanted to impose a kind of time-metered punishment system–in which specified infractions would be linked to a certain number of minutes of manual labor rather than to a general work-crew assignment–Sean warned that "we are not doing prison sentences here; these are kids, not adults." After one school manager repeatedly put himself within inches of students' faces and shouted expletives and racial epithets ("You look like a spic"), mimicking the image of a boot camp and threatening in fact to send students there, Sean had him transferred out. When a bus driver hit a student, he was fired–a sign of Sean's seriousness in the matter, since bus drivers were hard to come by. (Five men applying for a driver position earlier in the year had failed a urine drug test.)

For some months there were deliberations about "academic consequences." A few of the teachers thought students would work harder during class if they knew they could be made to stay after school to finish academic unit work. Sean at first turned this down, saying, "It's probably not a good idea if schoolwork feels like punishment." But in the spring, just before the annual inspection from the state juvenile justice agency, teachers received a memo announcing a "Corrective Action Plan" to increase the rate at which students were acquiring school credit. Of twelve students nearing the point of finishing the program that month, eight had acquired three or fewer credits, with most of the credits coming from nonacademic courses such as life skills and physical education. Two of the students had been in the program a year and a half–three times longer than what was promised by school policy–but had earned fewer than two credits each. A productivity chart was distributed indicating the number of credits earned in each teacher's class, stapled along with a note from Kevin that "the ratio of incompletion is unsatisfactory." Teachers were advised to submit weekly the names of students not "completing academic expectations" and authorized to apply a new range of consequences for sluggish classroom performance. These included mandatory weekend classes, which some of the hourly-wage staff volunteered to supervise, and an after-school academic work-crew assignment. "We are a school," Sean said at the meeting where the action plan was introduced. "Our job is to make sure the students get those credits."

But the teachers felt their hands had been tied: earlier that very week, Ed, the assistant director, had cautioned them, as he did periodically, not to "overuse" the consequence work crews. The large number of students needing his attention during these work assignments, he warned, was tying up his schedule and slowing the other operations of the school. "I won't come after them if you send them around the corner," he said. "I'll come and see you."

Pressured from above to enhance productivity, constrained from below by many students' disinclination to give their hearts to boring assignments that provided little intrinsic reward, teachers had available to them few of the devices to which their counterparts in larger or more traditional public schools might resort. They couldn't force large numbers of students out of the classroom, since Ed disapproved of it and limited personnel resources made it impractical. They had no intermediary on whom to blame low productivity or bad student behavior, since the school was small enough that every teacher could be held personally and directly responsible for shortcomings in performance in his or her own classroom. The prevailing official ideology, upheld by Sean, banned corporal punishment and other forms of physical coercion as well as public humiliation of students, so these long-standing features of juvenile justice, as well as of some public schools in the region, were unavailable. Sean was demanding even-handedness, so teachers had to avoid any show of excessive caprice or vindictiveness in the grading of points and imposition of consequences. Sean's opinion of their work, moreover, was their sole source of job security and the primary determinant of pay raises.

Mitigating the Market System

In an effort to shield themselves from scrutiny and improve their situation,[3] teachers most of the time tended, despite Sean's and Ed's repeated calls for "teamwork" and "cooperation," to opt for privacy, not reporting the more embarrassing or potentially incriminating incidents they encountered during class. They kept their mishaps secret. After taking his class on a brief field trip, for example, Travis discovered upon returning to school that the students had stolen a screwdriver from the vocational classroom and drilled golfball-sized holes in several seat covers in the van. He never reported the damage. Some days later, when it was discovered by a bus driver, Sean was unable to convince anyone to speculate on how or when the holes had appeared, and under whose charge. On another occasion, when some students reportedly sprayed each other with fire extinguishers and an ambulance had to be called for one of the girls, who apparently had had an allergic reaction to the spray, a few staff insisted at first that the devices had "gone off by themselves," even though there had been a recent building-wide fire-code inspection and all the extinguishers had been found in satisfactory condition. When students turned up the thermostat in one of the fish tanks in the oceanography classroom, killing an expensive turtle, Laura kept quiet. Rick never told anyone when students in his class used a stick to bludgeon the head off a snake they'd captured in the creek alongside school property. Dwayne watched several students buying cigarettes from vagrants relaxing near a dock where the class was launching canoes; he never mentioned it. Kevin had seen several students throw fast-food packaging into the animal cages at the city zoo when he took them there on a Friday rec trip; he never reported it, and in fact announced as his afternoon "Staff Positive" later that day that he felt happy to have met the new students. In math and English, the daily routines of sleeping and hair twisting went virtually without comment. Teachers were told "fuck you" almost daily and were the brunt of obscene gestures and hostile threats ("I'll come to your house tonight"). The vast majority of these incidents went unreported and unremarked; the less badgering they did in response to minor infractions, the less risk teachers faced of having a small, relatively quiet incident escalate into a loud confrontation that could attract attention.

The school's official symbolic economy of ranks and points rested on a model of students as contract-signing agents who could be held responsible for their actions and punished or rewarded appropriately and systematically for their chosen decisions. Yet teachers clung to a notion as well that the students might be viewed occasionally as victims, worthy not only of blame and punishment but also perhaps of pity and forgiveness–that they were sometimes deserving, in other words, of the kind of break a teacher could give. Time and again, staff reminded themselves of circumstances that called for leniency and warmth instead of literalism or strictness in application of the rules. These reminders enabled them to assert for themselves the right to impose their own judgments, to make of themselves something more than mere technicians enforcing an immutable exchange system handed down by others. It was a means by which to claim, in certain contexts, an authority greater than that of the unit system and the behavioral rules intended to enforce it.[4]

Particularly when they sensed trouble at a student's home, they could become less harsh in applying sanctions or generous in distributing rewards. When a boy's mother disappeared in flight from police, for example, and his father was arrested and hauled off to the county jail, staff discussed the case at a meeting. The boy had been "acting out," as the teachers characterized it–cursing, sleeping through his classes, ignoring instructions, glaring at other students and even visitors. But nobody wanted to send him on a work crew for every infraction. "There's a lot of pressure on him right now," said Ed. "Let's keep that in mind for a while." When a girl caring for a relative's baby got into several fights at school, at one point rather seriously assaulting another student, staff decided at a meeting not to call the police. "We need to be careful," one said. "She's got twenty people living in that tiny house, and her father doesn't want her or the baby there." Staff agreed to "go easy," allowing her to stay in school until state juvenile justice workers could relocate her to another program several weeks later. One boy moved into the city homeless shelter after his father refused to let him in the house. He got into a number of heated arguments with staff that week, but word got around quickly; staff agreed "to work with him this week until he gets through" this. A girl whose mother was in prison was frequently allowed to leave her classes to visit Ed, whom she seemed to regard as a confidante. Sometimes, to spend time with her, Ed passed a variety of pressing administrative duties to the office manager or school secretary, much to the annoyance of the rest of the staff. One day, Sean said: "You've got to realize that when these kids say 'Fuck you, you son of a you know what,' what they're really saying is, 'Help me, pay attention to me, show me some affection and support.' You've got to understand the language of these kids. Consider the situation they're in, what they're really saying to you."

Deviations from official policy did not come free of cost, and teachers frequently had to defend themselves from the wrath of students who felt injustices had been done to them as a result of staff discretionary authority. One day, for example, during a hearing determining which students would earn rank promotions, the staff reviewed a request submitted by Debbie, a boisterous girl who had been in the program for several months but had been languishing on the lowest-rank bench. A loud-voiced girl "with a record this thick"—as she frequently boasted—of school code violations and legal trouble, she broke curfew virtually routinely and had been assigned to a work crew at least once each week for angry bouts of cursing and curfew violations. Still, Debbie had made what staff regarded unanimously as "remarkable progress" in her "social skills" and "self-control." She had finished several units in oceanography and was close to earning a class credit; there were no new formal law violations; articulate and never shy, having been active in the drama club back at the regular high school, she had even been chosen to lead some visitors on a tour of the school. "She has come so far," said a teacher. "She is much better than she was a couple of months ago." Others agreed: "There is no comparison in her attitude, in her attendance. We need to acknowledge that." Debbie was granted a promotion to the next rank. At lunch, beaming, she took her seat on a new bench in the assembly hall. Teachers felt confident they had done the right thing.

The same day, however, Erique came up for promotion. Strictly speaking, Erique had earned the points he needed for a rank increase: he'd easily finished several units in math and English the previous few weeks and had not broken curfew even once. He'd kept quiet, hadn't fought with anyone, and had volunteered frequently in morning and afternoon assemblies, leading the "Pledge" and the "Prayer" and on several occasions offering "Positive Thoughts." Though they had no tangible evidence, however, the staff believed Erique had been circulating cigarettes among the students; one thought he recognized Erique's handwriting on graffiti on a school table. A juvenile justice caseworker, moreover, suspected Erique of dealing drugs from home. The teachers acknowledged his "achievements" but denied his promotion request. "You're not there yet," he was told in his hearing. "We want you to do better than you're doing; and we know you can do it."

At lunch, Erique discovered that Debbie had been promoted. He was furious. "How many days was she on [work crew]?" he shouted, disrupting the distribution of the lunches. "Many days. How many was I on [work crew]? Not as many. It's not right. You have different standards." Erique stomped his feet from class to class the rest of the day; he made snorting noises at teachers and called the bus driver a "faggot"; he knocked over a desk in one of the classrooms and pulled the plug on the candy machine in the assembly hall. "This fucking place," he said. "They just mess with you."

"Worry about yourself," Kevin had said, "not about Debbie." But the next morning Erique didn't show up to school. When his mother finally brought him in some hours later, he spoke to no one and ignored the staff when they greeted him.

Keesha was another challenging student. An unwed mother reading at the second-grade level, she'd been assigned to Academy for knifing her abusive boyfriend in the stomach during a fight. She was the subject of frequent conversations among the staff, who considered her among the neediest of their charges, emotionally and academically. Keesha never skipped a day at Academy and often "made rec." Too shy and uncertain of her speaking abilities to volunteer for assemblies, she nevertheless appeared always to work diligently and quietly in her classes. Other students sometimes teased her about her clothes, which often were dirty, and her appearance–"you fat ugly mama." But Keesha over the months managed to keep to herself, restrain her temper, and make every apparent effort to finish the program. Staff encouraged her with rewards of field trips and fast-food meals, which she eagerly accepted. They complimented her on her hair and occasional efforts to dress up for school. Staff marveled during meetings about "how far she's come." But since Keesha could barely read, her schoolwork was a sham. Day after day, she copied questions straight from her workbooks and wrote out instructions, virtually word for word, on her sheets of looseleaf paper. In math she never solved problems; she only copied them from the book. In English she never circled nouns or filled in verbs; she merely rewrote the worksheet sentences, leaving the blanks still empty. The teachers knew what was happening; Kevin said there were not enough personnel in the school to provide her with steady support. Eventually, Keesha earned enough points for promotion to the top rank, and staff decided to let her graduate Academy with a formal ceremony even though she'd earned none of the required school credits and her test-score gains were minimal. "This will be so important to her," they agreed, and one of the community liaisons was assigned the challenge of helping her develop and present a brief graduation speech. Other students, however, complained:

"She ain't got no credits, but she still be graduating," said one, shaking her head in disgust.

"She be staring at people; what kind of attitude is that?" said another."

"I see her in math," complained a third. "She just write the question; she don't get the answer. She write eight plus one, eight plus one, like that, over and over. She ain't doing what she supposed to do–they still let her out. That ain't fair."

"They be bragging about her that she ain't miss a day (of school), she come in every day. Next time they say that I'll be raising my hand."

On a day-to-day level, teachers sought to make the school a place they could themselves at least partly enjoy, and they organized many school activities around their own personal interests; staff ties to the community, in fact, were the sole means of developing and enriching the school program. Sherry, for instance, took the students on field trips to the local Urban League, where she had an affiliation, to hear lectures about women's issues. Before Christmas, a time of year when police generally reported increasing rates of arrest of teenagers caught shoplifting or stealing cash from parked cars—a source of money for gift-buying—staff worried about diverting students from petty crime, and Travis arranged for a group of top performers to work a few days on the farm where he lived. They earned $5 an hour for clearing brush and mending fences in the pecan orchard. Kevin convinced a hunting partner to donate several wild ducks to Rick's ethnic cooking project. Laura took students to lectures at the university. Marcus shared from home a book about famous black Americans from which students occasionally excerpted "Positive Thoughts" to offer during assembly.

Adding Meaning to the Workplace

Though most staff were aware that teachers "are not supposed to talk about religion," as one put it, they nonetheless introduced religious themes, speeches, and activities throughout the school program. Staff consistently endeavored to "do God's work" on the job, as Kevin referred to it. Most of the staff, it will be remembered, were evangelical Christians—there were a church deaconess, two ordained ministers, a seminary graduate with ties to the Moral Majority, a Christian academy graduate, and a self-proclaimed born-again Christian—and they conceived of their work in distinctly religious terms, as a kind of "calling" or ministry. This made it possible for them to imbue an oftentimes frustrating work environment with great moral meaning and significance; it also provided an outlet for distancing themselves from some of the more personally troubling aspects of the institution and the work.

Sean, for example, kept a Bible on his office desk. On several occasions when visitors were in the building, he placed his hand on it and announced: "This is where I get the rules to run this program." During an assembly, Sherry said that in a church service she had attended she suddenly "realized that this is the job God wanted for me." Rick told students that he had come to Academy "because the Lord prevailed in me" when it came time to decide on a career change. "This is my real ministry," said William, one of the community liaisons who was also an ordained Baptist minister. "I can minister in [my] church, but this is where I have the close contact with kids, where I can really minister to them. We can't be too direct about religion because of, you know, the state, but we can teach values and behavior and that kind of thing. I consider this a chance to really minister to kids."

Cindy quoted scripture frequently in class, sometimes played gospel music softly on a tape player as the students worked at their seats, and, in place of the officially emblazoned Academy logo shirts that teachers were asked to wear to work, frequently wore t-shirts printed with the names of church conventions she had attended or with religious-oriented slogans ("Be Right With Jesus or Be Left," for example). She often wrote messages on her classroom dry-erase board: "What you are is God's gift to you . . . what you do with yourself is your gift to God." Or "He who has no dreams shall perish.–The Word." Marcus joined her in the habit of keeping a Bible on his classroom desk. Scriptural quotations–excerpts from the Book of Matthew were popular–occasionally appeared on such official documents as class schedules. Sean sometimes signed his memoranda with the phrase "God Bless" and one day distributed among staff a copy of a newspaper editorial someone had sent him touting the power of prayer to curtail juvenile drug use.

In the spring, when the state branch of the Christian Coalition, the right-wing religious and lobbying organization, sponsored a prayer rally on the steps of the state capitol building to support a legislative bill allowing prayer in public schools, Academy students were bused to the capitol to participate, accompanied by Cindy and Rick. Cindy met some church friends there, they led a prayer together, and unprecedented high scores were distributed among the students' point cards. When Sean and Ed arranged for a school visit from a prison ministry, students got to leave classes to watch a performance of weightlifting and basketball tricks, accompanied by exhortations from the performers: "God is working through me. . . . The only person who can turn your life around is Jesus."

Every day began for teachers with a prayer at the morning staff meeting. Standing in a circle, sometimes holding hands, other times stretching them toward the center like the spokes of a wheel, all the teachers started their day by closing their eyes while one, usually Cindy, the English teacher, recited a few lines of prayer. The prayers generally were a variation of: "Lord, thank you for sending us your Son so we can experience your love and know your plan for us." Or "Lord, help us to do what you have in store for us this day." The others would follow in unison with "Amen."

The notion of having been called to a ministry provided a standpoint from which staff could criticize both the juvenile justice system whose front lines they embodied as well as certain features of the surrounding cultural milieu from which they wanted to distance themselves. Social and legal injustices perpetrated against the students in their charge, the kind of brutality and irrationality pervasive in the students' lives and in the juvenile justice system, were a topic of frequent conversation and lamentation, and during meetings and on training days, staff exchanged "horror stories" about overly punitive judges, vindictive police, or cruel public school personnel, contrasting their own moral endeavors with what they regarded as the wrongs committed by others. They could in this way be both a part of the system and apart from it.

There was considerable irritation, for example, when a very young boy who had just completed the program and returned to public school was re-arrested and saddled with new charges. The crime: skipping school one day and getting caught carrying an unopened bottle of beer. Staff felt an arrest in this case was overly harsh; the matter could have been handled in other ways. One student whose family was in a particularly difficult financial situation was caught one morning apparently prostituting for breakfast money; a few staff wondered together why the police who found her had rushed her to the juvenile booking center. "They could've just brought her back here," said a teacher. There was considerable aggravation when staff learned that a one-time student who had been considered a success, landing a steady job and earning a high-school equivalency diploma, had been arrested for having a girlfriend who was underage. Though parents of both partners approved of the relationship, the story in the staff room went, a judge had sentenced the boy to five years in an adult prison. "There's something wrong with this system," said a staff member. "You try and try, and then something like this happens. It's crazy. What kind of message are these kids getting?" When one student returned, as he'd hoped, to regular high school but was expelled after several days of absenteeism, which staff reasoned was related to his parents' having fled from a police drug raid on their house, staff shook their heads in disgust: "Why they do something like that?"

In the spring, reporters, television news crews, and civil rights activists from around the world descended on the city as news reports circulated that white administrators of a church in one of the surrounding rural towns had demanded the disinterment from the church cemetery of a biracial baby who had died soon after birth. Like many others in the city, staff accepted the news with a mixture of anguish and embarrassment. At a meeting one afternoon, they grappled collectively with its meaning. Four teachers, independently of one another, had attended race-reconciliation activities sponsored by their churches in the wake of the news. Marcus described how his black pastor had "opened up honestly about his negative feelings toward whites." Travis reported on the "guilt" he'd felt after attending a men's prayer breakfast where the subject of the sermon was white treatment of blacks. Sharing their personal experiences, they reiterated a collective commitment to a spiritual equality apparently absent from the world outside the school. "When He come," Michael, the community liaison, said, "He don't see the color of your skin. He don't see black or white or brown. He don't see the money in your bank account; you rich or poor. He don't see the property you own, the size of your car or your house. He see what's in your heart. That's what He look at."

"Amen," said several of the others.

It is morning. Dwayne is setting out on a boating trip with his class; the van is full, the trailer in back loaded down with canoes. Short of cash to buy fishing bait, Dwayne pulls the van into a bank drive-through. In the lane alongside us is a middle-aged white man in a high-end silver Mercedes. He is obviously angry; he is gesturing frantically at the teller, his hands in the air, his head shaking. It is obvious that he is shouting, but we cannot hear what is being said because the van windows are closed. The students watch attentively, their eyes fixed on an unfolding temper tantrum the likes of which could land any of them, easily, in the juvenile detention center.

"He drive a Mercedes," Erica, a student, says finally. "He think he have a right to yell when he want, at whoever he mad at." There are nods all around. One of the students shakes his head in disgust.

In the afternoon, after the students have left school, Dwayne relates the scene to the other staff. "You should have seen the man," he says. "And in a silver Mercedes."

"Bless their hearts," Cindy says.

Religion as an Indicator of Program Success

Teachers aimed to "turn kids' lives around," in school parlance. To this end, they went beyond mundanely asserting that program goals had been achieved as soon as points and rank had been acquired. Rather, in conversations and gestures, amid pervasive religious imagery and language, they cast student stories as narratives of redemption and rebirth. The primary vehicle for these characterizations was the graduation ceremony, which followed generally the outlines of a traditional Christian evangelical conversion narrative (Hall and Stack 1982; Williams 1982). Moving rhetorically from sin to salvation, graduations were a ritual of transformation, connecting the practical program methodology of point acquisition to the school's higher but more operationally elusive educational and rehabilitative mission. Such rituals gave definition to teachers' daily labors and made it possible to claim, despite the more narrowly economistic nature of the prevailing point system, that something special had been accomplished with all that work.

Graduation ceremonies were held on Friday afternoons near the end of each month, except during the summer. The names of graduating students were announced several weeks ahead of time during morning assembly, and students were reminded that soon-to-be-graduates were going to have to work extra hard the next few weeks in order to stay out of trouble, finish any lingering classwork, secure those last few behavioral points, and keep up attendance. Each month, between one and seven students acquired the requisite number of points and school credits for graduation and found a job or school placement. The morning of graduation, students assigned to "consequence" work crews would mop the floors and sponge down the benches in the assembly hall. One of the community liaisons would order cake and fruit platters from a supermarket nearby and check the kitchen cabinets to make sure there were enough paper cups and plates.

The ceremony would begin after lunch. Family members were always invited. Caseworkers from the state juvenile justice agency and social workers from the police department often attended; occasionally there were observers from a university, and sometimes one of the local retired judges would come with a variety of guests. Staff dressed formally in suits and ties or dresses, and the rest of the students were asked to wear Academy-logo t-shirts in the color signifying their rank (these were usually distributed the afternoon before graduation day); wearing them could earn a student four points in the "Appearance" section of the point card. Graduations had special seating arrangements. Usually organized into rows representative of rank, the benches would be arrayed in a rectangle around the perimeter of the assembly hall; in the center, folding chairs were set up for the visitors; at the front was a podium. Students sat in benches according to homeroom class and advisor rather than according to rank, and the teachers joined them there.

The ceremony consisted of five parts–the opening, the awards, the sermon/prayer, the graduation speech, and the celebration meal marking the reunification of graduates with the community. As the crowd settled into their seats, the graduates-to-be would be assembled at the closet in the conference room, where they sorted through the school's collection of blue-satin graduation gowns and caps, each student choosing one that fit. When the graduates were dressed, Ed would call out their names, one by one, and they would file into the assembly hall to sit in folding chairs arranged in a row at the front of the room, facing the visitors. Two or three high-ranking students would then take turns at the podium, welcoming the visitors or reading excerpts from books or poetry.

The teachers would then proceeded to the front of the hall, stopping briefly to shake hands with each graduate. Standing alongside Ed, each teacher would announce student awards for the month, calling out the names of the winners. There were awards from each teacher for best attendance, best classroom performance, and "most improved" student. Dwayne, the boating teacher, gave the award for "Angler of the Month." Some months, awards had religious themes: Cindy, for example, gave something she titled "Ram in the Bush Award." (It was not clear whether the students actually understood the reference to the biblical story of opportunity.) Homerooms with the best attendance would be announced, usually by Ed, and promised a free restaurant lunch. As their names were called, students would rise from the benches and make their way to the front of the hall, some beaming, others shyly hesitant, some waving and smirking to cheers from the others. Certificates were given, on which winners' names had been written in calligraphic marker by the school receptionist. Teachers shook hands with each of the winners; staff and students alike cheered and clapped.

Teachers would then return to the benches, and students quieted down. Then Ed would announce the invited guest who would lead the sermon and prayer. Over the months, these guests had included a retired professional football player who was now a Christian motivational speaker, a local Baptist church leader, a lawyer, one of the school's own employee ministers, and one of the school's assistant directors, who had taken a Dale Carnegie class in public speaking (and who later scuffled with some students, for which Sean had him transferred out of the program). The sermons usually lasted about twenty minutes, during which the students would be admonished to "pray to Jesus to deliver you" from "the devil" or told to "go to Jesus; you can't do it by yourself." One speaker's theme was: "Choose ye this day whom you will serve." He led the students in gender-segregated prayers, alternating boys, who had to stand and repeat "I am a man of valor, I am courageous, I am trustworthy," with girls, who said, "I am a woman of value, I keep myself, I respect myself." With the exception of the lawyer's speech, which lasted more than half an hour on the topic of "agape love" and during which students had several times to be disciplined to sit still, the speeches followed a call-and-response pattern, the kind typical of preacher-congregation interactions in the local black Baptist churches. Students and staff alike tended to chime in periodically with "Amen," "Tell it,

tell it," "Yes, brother," or "The Truth." With the exception of
the lawyer, speakers emphasized a common bond of sin and
struggle uniting teachers and students, noting similarities
between the salvation of the staff and the potential salvation
of the students. The Christian motivational speaker, for example, reported that he had had run-ins with the law before
"finding Jesus," and the school's assistant director described
his upbringing with eleven siblings in a rural sharecropper
cabin with no plumbing. The school's community liaison-
minister gave a particularly rousing speech for which he
received a standing ovation. "I know there are kids here who
cry at night because of what they don't have," he said. "You
don't have to tell me it's hard, it hurts. I grew up in the projects. I know how hard it is. But I made a choice. You can
make a choice. It is up to you to turn your life around."

At the close of the prayer/speech, Ed or Sean would return
to the front of the assembly hall and thank the speaker. Sean
occasionally would add a few words of his own, cautioning
students, for example, that "the devil is just waiting for you
to make bad decisions." One month he told them: "I've been
locked up; I know you can break out of that cycle."

Then came the students' graduation speeches. About a
week before the ceremony, soon-to-be graduates were given
a "Graduation Speech Guide Sheet," a five-part outline
detailing the information staff wanted to see included in each
student's speech. These were organized around the format
of abbreviated conversion narratives:

I. Talk about your life before you came to Academy.
    A. Were you going to school?
    B. Were you getting into a lot of trouble? If yes, dis-
        cuss this.

    C. Were you hanging around positive or negative friends?

II. Talk about how you felt about Academy once you started the program.
    A. Were you happy to be here?
    B. Did you come to school regularly?
    C. What experience or experiences do you remember?
    D. Were there any staff members you really liked or that made a strong impact on you? If yes, who and what did they do?

III. Talk about what you have learned from being at Academy.
    A. Do you respect yourself and others more?
    B. Are you showing more respect for your parents and family at home?
    C. Have you improved your educational level?

IV. Talk about what you plan to do now.
    A. Where have you placed: adult ed, back to high school, or the high school credit program?
    B. Do you have a job or do you plan to get a job?
    C. What do you want to be doing 2 years from now: college, trade school, etc.?

V. Add anything that you would like to say relating to your speech or your time at Academy.

Student speeches would last about five minutes. Students would begin, following the outline given to them, by attesting to the evil and sin prevailing in their lives before the Academy experience:

    I used to get into fights.

> I got arrested by a narc.
>
> I wasn't going to school.
>
> I was hanging around with the wrong people.

The narrative would continue with descriptions of painful moments of self-realization:

> At first I hated it here.
>
> I was bucking, running.
>
> It was hard in the beginning; I didn't think I was going to like it.

They moved then to testimony of the infusion of some kind of grace, usually in the form of new-found family harmony or school credits:

> I got five and a half credits.
>
> I stopped fighting with my parents.

In the culminating moments, graduates would offer evidence of having begun a new and transformed life:

> I'm going back to school.
>
> I'll be graduating with my class next summer.
>
> I want to go to college and become a paramedic.

At the close of the speeches, staff and students would clap, and then Ed, standing at the front of the hall, would congratulate the graduates as the female staff members arranged the food and plates on a buffet table behind him. Ed would then announce that it was time to eat. He invited visitors and graduates from the folding chairs to be first at the food line at the buffet table, followed by students in the benches closest to the front, then those sitting farther back, and so on, until everyone was lined up. Eating lasted about twenty minutes, and then graduates would be allowed to go home with visiting relatives, if any had come (they not always did). The rest of the students were then dismissed to homeroom to prepare for boarding the vans.

The redemption narratives of the graduation ceremony, guided as they were by staff input, connected the practical operational details of students' daily school experiences to a system of outcomes meaningful to staff and within the reach of what staff felt able realistically to accomplish. Unable for a variety of reasons to equip students with authentic academic and vocational skills, they offered in place of these a ceremony celebrating religious renewal and official passage into a new life.[5]

Severing from the Pain of Responsibility

For all their efforts to make the school a morally significant place from which to derive personal satisfaction and a sense of accomplishment, teachers could, when they wanted to, sever themselves from what was regarded universally as the most difficult and painful aspect of the job. When students failed the program or completed it successfully only to be re-arrested soon after—sometimes appearing on the evening news in handcuffs while being maneuvered by uniformed men into the back seats of police cars—staff had available to them explanations that did not point solely to their own shortcomings or to those of the school. They could claim, often with good evidence, that some of the students were simply too sick, too violent, or not a good match for the school regimen prescribed for them.

There was a major trial in this regard in the case of Andre, who had been in the program for some months and had been doing relatively well, by most accounts. He had won an award for "Student of the Month" in one class, and staff at meetings had talked about "attitude improvements" accompanying his move out of a crack den and into his grandmother's house. Andre was scheduled to finish Academy and be placed in a job or continuing education class. But one night as his last school day approached, Andre reportedly kicked a man nearly to death after a neighborhood basketball game. As his victim languished in the hospital intensive-care unit, Andre hid. He later turned himself in and was arrested on charges of attempted first-degree murder. He'd be tried as an adult. The story made opening headline news on all the local television stations, and the following morning Andre's picture topped the local pages of the city paper. At their morning meeting, staff deliberated in sadness and regret. But in the end, they were able to negotiate a kind of rhetorical retelling of the boy's experience in the program, agreeing, ultimately, that Andre had been to begin with a strange and difficult student and perhaps not right for what Academy had to offer:

Cindy: He did that while he was in the program, and we didn't even know about it.

Carol: We thought he was a good student. How do you explain that?

Travis: That was the behavior he displayed when he was here. We can't know what he's doing when he's not here.

Michael: He kept to himself, very quiet. Those are the ones you have to worry about. The ones who go along and keep to themselves, but you never know what is going on in their heads.

Dwayne: He was a strange kid. He beat up Rafael so violently on the van one day, and then he went into the house and got a paper towel for Rafael to wipe the blood off his face and the van walls and ceiling. It was weird.

Cindy: He couldn't control his temper. There's a fine line between sanity and insanity. Maybe that's why we couldn't tell.

Dwayne: I even gave him an award this month. [Everyone laughs.]

Marcus: He's going to jail now.

Michael: We're getting too many kids who don't belong in the program. Louis doesn't belong here, and some others, too.

Marcus: But we take them. Perry doesn't belong here.

Cindy: Why do you say that?

Marcus: He got coked up, kidnapped three girls, and then drove to Georgia to try to kill his father. Perry ain't as nice as he looks.

Michael: But we take them. We just bring them in here.

Sherry: You can't save every kid.

Market Tensions

Pressured by their supervisors to enhance classroom productivity yet held to certain strictly enforced standards of humane behavior, and confronted daily with student boredom and defiance, teachers found themselves ever grappling with the limitations and frustrations of the school's prevailing market system of merit. Like their students, they developed strategies by which to mitigate market rigidities, circumvent the discipline of their supervisors, make their daily labors more rewarding, and invest their work with personal meaning and significance beyond what was available through the simple exchange of symbolic commodities. They kept their mishaps secret, distanced themselves from particularly troublesome problems, and asserted the authority to deviate from official rules governing the price and distribution of rewards and punishments. There were limits, in other words, to the reach of the school's prevailing economic logic. Max Weber (1976), the sociologist, saw that marketplace principles penetrate deeply into personal psychology, that bureaucracy and competitiveness shape the very core of modern consciousness. But no caring teacher could treat every student with a bureaucratic sameness; unbendable regulations would be pointlessly harsh. Among staff, the imperative to care for students intruded on the call for consistency in the application of market rules and the management of productivity at work.

Religion figured centrally in teachers' work. Evangelical religion has a unique centrality in Southern cultural and political life; the lines separating church from state in the South differ from those typical of other parts of the nation (Hunter 1983; Flake 1984; Wilson 1995; Kosmin and Lachman 1993; Grantham 1994). For evangelicals, religion is active and not contemplative; schooling is a means to God's ends. Staff regarded their work as a ministry; they endowed the school in this way with moral value and invested themselves with a power and importance beyond what was available through small salaries and limited official decision-making authority. As evangelicals, they stressed the spiritual unity and equality of all people and pointed to conditions and experiences common to staff and students alike, even as they made the students attend right-wing, religion-oriented political rallies.

Troubled children are a big business in America; an army of professional experts awaits them at every life stage. Each professional group has a way of talking scientifically about its concerns, its objectives, and its claims of specialization. Educators concern themselves with classroom disruptiveness and learning difficulties. Social workers worry about substance abuse and family relations. Psychologists worry about poorly developed interpersonal skills and low self-esteem; clinical therapists focus on behaviors they perceive as symptoms of underlying family or individual pathology. Children are carved up into domains of accountability; their social and psychological problems are measured as so many deficits and disabilities, so many deviations from the norm and degrees distant from the professional ideal.[6] Deriving meaning and motivation from their religious faith, however, Academy staff made little connection with the "deficit" language and fragmented accountability of contemporary professional child-care culture. They embraced instead a definition of children as potentially prayerful and blessed with the capacity both for sin and for religious renewal; it was a holistic definition more in keeping with their understanding of themselves as "ministering."

Religious definitions were a key to teachers' sense of having achieved something worthwhile under difficult working conditions. Given limited resources and a limited curriculum and instructional methodology, staff could not claim that substantive and long-lasting inroads had been made in students' academic and vocational skills. Moreover, given the reality that a great deal of what happened to students legally, economically, and socially after they left the program was far beyond staff control, staff could not claim that they had secured just and lasting solutions to all their wayward charges' outstanding trials and troubles. But at the point of graduation, students indeed joined staff in ceremonially transforming their labor in acquiring points into a statement of having achieved at least some version of the school's higher mission. Graduation ceremonies and speeches connected the practical operational details of each student's Academy experience to the higher policy mission and philosophical imperative toward which the teachers ultimately had been hired to toil. Students themselves attested that transformations officially had taken place, that teachers' labors weren't for naught.

But even moralism had its limits. When students failed, explanations could be found that did not place the burden of responsibility on teachers' shoulders.

7

Measurement

FOR ALL THE INTENTIONS that had accompanied
Academy's opening, the work of measuring the school's
actual effects proved complex and contentious. It may be
said that the measurement of educational outcomes is
always fraught with difficulty; this is perhaps even more the
case for schools such as Academy, situated as they are
between multiple regulatory and management agencies. The
road to outcome and effectiveness measures was paved with
political obstacles and practical and methodological pitfalls.
Producing numbers to satisfy the oversight agencies became
for Academy managers an achievement in and of itself.

Formal measurement of Academy's effects focused primarily on recidivism, the matter of foremost concern to the state
juvenile justice agency and its program evaluators in search
of bottom-line indicators to deliver to legislators and dollar-
conscious taxpayers. Recidivism statistics were calculated by
Academy's parent firm as well as by state agencies, but there
was wrangling over access to the needed databases as well as
over how best to define and calculate the outcome measures.

The agency in charge of statewide criminal justice databases shared information with Academy's administrators

free of charge for several years but at one point decided, rather suddenly it was claimed by some school officials, to charge a considerable per-file fee. Academy officials subsequently had to go hunting for alternate and lower-cost sources of data. The state juvenile justice agency, eager for hard data so as to begin the systematic evaluations required by state law, offered as a stopgap measure to share at no charge the information its own employees had collected, but it was not clear that this would be a long-term arrangement. Data were not easily accessible or clear-cut at any rate: one agency kept track of children under age eighteen in terms of any formal referrals they had had with state social service workers, regardless of whether referrals resulted in any change in legal status; a different agency monitored conviction and imprisonment statistics for convicts age eighteen and over; a third kept information on convicts of any age who had found paid employment in a prison work program. All discussion of outcome statistics consequently had to be accompanied by lengthy cautions explaining a variety of sources of error, omission, or double counting.[1]

There was widespread policy disagreement over the best method by which to calculate recidivism. According to figures calculated by one state agency, fewer than 30 percent of Academy's successful completers were referred back into the juvenile justice system within a year of completing the program. This figure was very similar to those reported for other programs for "low-risk" youth in the state and considerably lower than what was reported by more punitive justice facilities such as boot camps, which tended to serve youth with a track record of more serious or repeat offenses. It was certainly in line with trends evident since the passage of federal juvenile justice reforms in the 1970s of apparently better outcomes for less punitive programs serving less violent youth (Bernard 1992). Academy personnel conducted their analysis in a different way, however, using data on arrests and convictions rather than on mere re-entry into the social service net; this methodological choice made the program's outcomes seem even more definitively and resoundingly positive, with somewhere between 10 and 20 percent of school completers getting re-arrested and convicted within the first year of their termination from the program.

The calculation of recidivism became increasingly controversial and contentious as state officials moved closer to their mandated goal of developing a cost-benefit analysis instrument that would guide decisions about which private program contracts to renew, cancel, or expand. Academy administrators worried, with good reason, that cost-benefit statistics would not adequately portray the nature of what actually happened qualitatively between students and staff in the program, and meetings of the state's juvenile justice oversight board were punctuated throughout the year by debates over the best way to calculate recidivism in relation to program costs.

At the level of the school itself, pressures on Sean and Ed to deliver favorable recidivism statistics entered into the matter of how to assign students to "favorable termination" or "unfavorable termination," the two broad categories into which Academy leavers were sorted and which formed the base lists from which recidivism ultimately was calculated. "Unfavorable termination" referred to students who were expelled from the school for violence, persistent misbehavior, or new legal violations. "Favorable termination" referred to two types of student: those eligible for graduation and those who had completed some but not all the purported graduation requirements. To be eligible for a full-fledged graduation ceremony, students had to reach the top rank through the point-card system, find a job or school placement, and earn at least two high school credits. According to the school handbook, students were also expected to earn certificates in CPR and first aid and raise by two grade levels their scores on a standardized academic achievement test. These latter rules were not enforced, however, since the school never had enough qualified staff to offer CPR and first-aid courses on a regular basis. A small number of students, moreover, did not achieve the called-for grade-level increase. In a thirteen-month period from 1995 to 1996, according to available data, fifty students were officially expelled from Academy–"unfavorably terminated"–mostly for reasons of violence, drug possession, absconding, or arrest. Sixty officially finished the program successfully– they were "favorably terminated"–with seventeen of these meeting the special requirements for a graduation ceremony.

White males were proportionately slightly more likely than other students to be among the graduates (n = 8). In several instances, however, Academy students scheduled for "favorable termination" had been demoted suddenly and in the last minute to "unfavorable" status after getting arrested or going into hiding just before the date they were to finish the program. In at least one instance, a well-liked student scheduled for a full-fledged graduation ceremony had been demoted to the "favorable termination" list after getting arrested, just before his graduation day, on a new law violation. On the other hand, a girl who refused to come to school for several weeks was not listed, as most such cases would be, as an "abscond," an "unfavorable termination" category. Staff regarded her as a bright and promising girl

who had had a difficult adolescence and an exceedingly troubled family life, but who nonetheless would succeed eventually in her future endeavors. Ed kept her on the school
rolls, making sure her home was contacted daily by phone
until the juvenile justice caseworker managed to line up an
alternative placement, at which point she was labeled a
"favorable termination."

Last-minute "adjustments" such as these in the statistical
image of students that school administrators presented in
their official reports to the outside world were greeted with
a mix of irony and empathy on the part of the local juvenile
justice administrator, who, to her credit, knew well the twists
and turns of each student's unique story and the struggles of
Academy staff to cope with what had been placed at their
doorsteps. "Get what you need to get–favorable, unfavorable," the caseworker had said at a meeting when staff were
discussing the case of the girl who wouldn't return to school.
"I don't care how you do it. I'm just trying to get the best possible placement for her."

The school did not keep aggregate enrollment figures in
the usual sense. It did not report enrollment totals, for example, for any period of months. Rather, there was an "open-
entry/open-exit" policy, with students arriving at a great
variety of points in the year, according to a schedule over
which staff had little control. There was no formal beginning
and no formal end to the school calendar. While teachers
could rattle off the names of students in their homeroom or
in any particular class, they kept no running log, either formal or informal, of the total number of students who had
passed through the doors during the year or over any other
stretch of time. Instead, daily attendance sheets were compiled; the school receptionist collated these each month into

a report to the state juvenile justice agency of that month's billable "client service days." The school district, for its part, received lists at roughly nine-week intervals with grades listed for students who had been in attendance.

Daily attendance ranged from twenty-five to fifty. While some students appeared for only a day and others lingered more than four hundred days, the average length of stay for successful completers was between six and seven months, matching the promises made in official school contracts with the state juvenile justice agency and the local public school district. A slightly shorter stay was reported, on average, for those who were expelled. Comparisons of data available on the length of stay of black students with the length of stay of whites, or that of females with that of males, revealed no systematic pattern.

There was a great deal of flexibility, as well as some institutional wrangling, in the way attendance was counted. Accounting in general reflected not only teachers' judgments and student achievement of official release criteria, but also administrators' timeliness and pressure on Sean and Ed, the school managers, to sustain a high reportable rate of attendance and successful program completion. Students on occasion were counted in attendance or as having had an "excused absence," for example, even when they had stayed home, as long as there had been phone contact. Conversely, there were instances in which students, usually at the beginning of their stay, apparently did not make the rolls even when they were in attendance, usually because admissions papers had not been filed on time. One month, some funding to the program reportedly was lost when a public school administrator from the district noticed that admissions forms had been filled out improperly and incompletely for a number of students; Kevin, the educational coordinator, complained bitterly about the districts' refusal to authorize payment for Academy's services to those students. Another month, when attendance was relatively low and a state inspection imminent, staff decided to increase the count of client service days by scheduling a weekend "community service workday" of tree planting and road maintenance. This project served both the school and its students, improving attendance statistics while also enabling some students to work off a few of the community service hours to which some of them had been sentenced. Staff maintained a general sense that they could at least to some degree "make the numbers what they need to be," as Ed characterized it in discussions with the teachers.

There was no ongoing or systematic monitoring of aggregate student academic achievement in the program. Summary statistics were not reported by the school, for example, on the total number of course credits earned during a year or over an interval of months; nor was there any systematic recording of the average number of course credits earned over any period or of the average length of time it took students to complete course credits. Teachers knew the names of the students who had earned credit in their classes and could count them in their heads if asked. But this knowledge was not organized or filed in such a way as to be readily retrievable. Grade lists were sent to the public school district according to a regular schedule, as contract specified. But when a student left the program, a final grade sheet would be forwarded to the appropriate district office, credits assigned by the district where appropriate, and another statistic relating a successful program completion merged with the statistics from other programs coming under the district's Dropout Prevention umbrella. Academy teachers generally had no occasion after a student left the program to revisit individual records in their own building or to extract from them any information that might be used to compile group statistics regarding what students had actually accomplished academically. Kevin, the academic coordinator, reported that his files were in a perpetual state of disarray and that it was practically impossible to retrieve any information on the academic achievement of students who had left the school either on favorable or unfavorable terms.

Moreover, after the point of their leaving, no agency or organization systematically monitored Academy completers' longer-term school academic experiences and outcomes. Statistics available from the local school district's Dropout Prevention administration indicated generally that many children in subcontracted juvenile justice programs never made it all the way to the point of public high school graduation.[2] But since numbers were reported for all programs combined, rather than for individual schools, there was no accounting on a program-by-program basis. Academy's official contract with the state juvenile justice agency specified in general terms that the school officials would monitor students' post-termination job and school placements and track them on a chart for at least two years. No personnel at the school had been assigned formally to this job, however; the receptionist during spare moments would place a phone call or two or mail brief questionnaires to terminated students' last known addresses. Little systematic data resulted from these efforts, and there was in the front office a thick file of returned questionnaires, dating back more than a year, with envelopes marked "Addressee Unknown."

Virtually all favorably terminated students and graduates left the program having finished what might become two public school credits if approved by the local school district supervisor. Virtually everyone in this category earned a potential half credit in the life skills class required for completion of the first two-week, after-school component of the program; most also earned at least half a credit, usually more, in some combination of vocational education, physical education, English or oceanography. These were not necessarily the minor achievements they might seem; they represented more measurable academic progress, at least in a strictly formal sense, than most students would have achieved had they dropped out of school entirely.

Testing in mathematics and reading was conducted at admission for all students and additionally at the point of program completion for graduates and, intermittently but not on a regular basis, for "favorably terminated" students other than those who had achieved criteria for graduation. The test being used at the time of the study was the Wide Range Achievement Test (WRAT), not known as an unequivocally effective measure of student achievement but favored in some contexts because it is easy and fast to administer. These revealed pre- and post-test skills changes similar to those reported by state officials for students in other juvenile justice programs where such tests are administered: while some students showed apparent skills decreases, improvements were evident in most cases, ranging up to seven grade levels and averaging around two. Sean almost always reported these statistics to visitors, for lack of other bottom-line academic indicators. The rest of the staff, however, like many observers in the state juvenile justice agency, put little stock in them. Kevin, who usually administered the tests, believed they reflected precisely the extent to which he would "whip [students] up" into enthusiasm just before the testing session. Michael, the community liaison who served as an alternate test administrator when Kevin was occupied, thought score increases reflected the calming effects of time; months had elapsed, in most cases, since test-takers' bitter and usually frenetic first weeks in the program after release from the overcrowded regional juvenile detention center.

Importantly, re-admission to public school was not automatic, even for the successful Academy completers who had achieved transferable school credits. It was the local public school district supervisor who made final decisions about student school re-entry. Academy staff had little or no authority in this area, though Kevin usually made a point of attending the monthly re-entry meetings where placement decisions were announced. A number of students hoping to return to one or another of the local public high schools were disappointed to find they would not be allowed back in, either because it was claimed enrollments there had already been capped or because district administrators simply preferred to place them in the public alternative "discipline" school for troubled teens or in a district-related continuing education program for adults. Staff were ambivalent about these placements, about which they maintained no aggregate data–disappointed, on one hand, because they wanted to see their successful students rewarded with the mainstream school re-entry placements they desired; relieved, on the other hand, because they harbored a sense that a large public high school might be a hostile and unsupportive environment, full of dangerous temptations, for returning students. Sean and Ed noted informally and with some frustration a feeling that fewer and fewer of their successful completers in recent months were being allowed back to the high school of their choice. Adult continuing education and

the local "last chance" school had become, they sensed, the
district administrator's favored placement sites, a situation
that in practice defined Academy not as a genuinely temporary alternative program that could feed successful students
back to the mainstream but rather as a kind of bottom layer
in the local status hierarchy of educational services. They
were gathering no systematic information to support or
refute this sense, however.

All favorably terminated students at Academy were
placed, as a condition of their release, in a job, school, or
other educational program (the adult literacy class at the
local Urban League, for example, was one such site), at least
temporarily, as a means of setting them on a path toward
productive adulthood. The jobs students secured after their
release were, in virtually all cases, of a low-paying nature
with limited prospects. School staff kept only vague job
placement records, usually noting only that a job had been
secured and not including in the records any information on
actual job title, position, or firm. From observations, however, it was apparent that busing tables, serving fast food, and
cashiering were the dominant job types. One boy took a job
as a gas station attendant, two as day laborers on construction sites, and a fourth as an assistant at the airport shoe-
shine shop. One student apparently found herself working
at a McDonald's where another student's mother was her
coworker. This made for considerable gossip, with students
debating whether their classmate's mother was to blame
when someone stole money out of the restaurant cash register in the middle of the day. With school or job placement
a condition of release, it was not uncommon for students to
tell friends and classmates that they had taken a particular
job "just so I can get out of here." No aggregate data were kept

on the average length of time students tended to keep these jobs, and staff knew that some students reported to their work placements only once or twice after leaving the program. Still, it was not uncommon for staff on their own time to pay occasional informal visits to the gas station or fast-food outlet where a favored graduate was known to be working, just to keep up contact and offer now and then a friendly greeting.

In the absence of legitimate and systematic educational outcome measures, there were measures related to the formal delivery of state-mandated educational services. All students at Academy received, officially at least, the 300 minutes of daily instructional time that were required by state oversight agencies for participants in Academy's particular category of the Dropout Prevention program. The pre-test administered on admission to the school, moreover, constituted at least some form of an official standardized academic assessment, also required by the state. These facts alone put Academy among the state's top-rated performers in terms of meeting legal mandates in education: overall, only 74 percent of young people in juvenile justice programs in the state the previous year had received the amount of daily instructional time required by law, and only 69 percent had had any academic assessment, according to data published by the state education agency. For all its problems, then, and despite the crude mediocrity of its educational programming, Academy ranked consistently among the state's top facilities in the area of education for juveniles in custody. For several years in a row it received from state juvenile justice inspectors ratings of "high" or "superior" in matters of educational funding, educational service delivery, educational personnel, transition planning, administration, and staff development.

Most of the students at Academy had spent more than a decade in public schools, yet many had come away unable to read or calculate with even a minimal degree of proficiency. They had arrived at the Academy front office carrying not only the bitterness of recent experience in "the system" but also the apparent emotional and physical scars of years of abuse and neglect. Academy was assigned the task of educating them, placing them in jobs as a condition of their release, and steering them away from crime–outcomes no other social or cultural institution in the city had managed in practice to achieve. In this context, it was not only methodologically but also politically difficult to design appropriate and meaningful outcome and effectiveness measures. Moreover, outcome and effectiveness statistics–scant, paltry, and subject to debate as they were–revealed comparatively little of what actually took place on a daily basis. Official statements of policy and program methodology were similarly lacking, since deviations from formally approved procedures were routine and pervasive and a distinct social system prevailed that was not described in any policy manual or handbook but that nonetheless had consequences and implications for students and staff alike.

The absence of clearly defined effectiveness measures reflects and reinforces what criminologist Mark Jacobs (1990) has called "the no-fault system." The contemporary rhetoric of tough-on-crime justice stresses that people should take responsibility for their actions. But both the juvenile justice system and the public schools are structured in a way that enables people in authority to avoid taking much of the blame when there is evidence of widespread failure. Judges and justice workers can say there was a shortage of space in appropriate programs for children, and they wouldn't be wrong. The governor can blame the legislature for money shortfalls, and he wouldn't be wrong. The legislature can say the public won't pay for needed facilities and services, and this would not be untrue. Caseworkers can point to parents and the myriad emotional and psychological problems that afflict juveniles in custody. Parents can point to schools. Schools can point to community disorder and resource limitations. Even the best-intentioned teachers can claim, with justification, that a student was simply too far gone, too low in skills and self-esteem, and too hard to reach by the time they finally got to him or her. The result of the "no-fault" system, as Jacobs notes, is to place the onus of responsibility on the student, who becomes the one on whom the full force and effects of social and institutional failure ultimately rest.

8

Conclusions

ACADEMY STUDENTS ARRIVED at the school having passed through an educational system characterized by low funding, low student achievement, harsh discipline, and evidence of ongoing racial inequity. They had come for the most part from environments of poverty and family strife. Some had close family members in prison. Several suffered severe chronic illnesses or infectious diseases, such as tuberculosis and hepatitis, and many carried physical scars of serious personal trauma. There was evidence of devastating emotional upheaval: the girls sucked their thumbs and fondled their ears like babies; some of the boys were given to bouts of withdrawal or muttering and sudden bursts of fury. Previous public schooling had failed to equip them with minimal competencies: many came without even functional literacy; confronting math problems, a few still counted on their fingers.

The students had entered a juvenile justice system characterized, despite recent efforts at reform and modernization, by ongoing processing delays, overcrowding, apparently capricious decision-making, indications of gender and racial bias, and in some cases physical violence. Judges and caseworkers had transformed students' specific law violations into official labels of delinquency necessitating specialized services in a state-approved treatment facility. A private facility affiliated with educational and justice agencies at state as well as local levels, Academy, like a growing number of institutions for delinquent children, was administratively positioned within a continuum of local public educational programs and services. But there was no avoiding the fact that its students were situated precariously on a rung of the ladder of escalating legal sanctions leading potentially to prison. The threat was always looming, as teachers and students were ever aware, of getting farther along in a justice system despised by so many.

The people who sought to work with these troubled and troubling children were, for the most part, idealistic and young, at a stage in their lives when they could give generously, as most did, of their time and energy. These were not traditional teachers: many had come from backgrounds of poverty and personal struggle, religion played an important role in the lives of most, and a higher percentage were black than is the case for most schools. Yet despite the high hopes and ambitions with which most tended to start the job, few lasted much longer than a year. Low pay, minimal training and benefits, no job security, and a sense of being under immense daily pressure to perform beyond the call of duty led to extremely high rates of staff turnover.

The school building itself reflected to some degree the prevailing ambivalence with which policymakers regard troubled children, embodying at once the harshness of recent tough-on-crime rhetoric as well as the high hopes with which Americans have historically embraced the idea of universal schooling. Alongside a general optimism about what might be done for children in custody, evident in Academy's array of brightly colored motivational banners and boating and diving equipment, was a sparseness of resources and thoughtful financial commitment, reflected daily in the absence of traditional school supplies and materials and in the state of nagging disrepair and disuse in which much of the equipment was kept.

In its techniques for managing student behavior, Academy had as its central organizing feature a token economy of rewards and payments with roots in nineteenth-century American penitentiary management principles, themselves drawn from Lancasterian strategies for the schooling of children of the poor. Students had to display compliance with institutional work rules in order to earn points, merit awards, and rank increases that served as a kind of currency with which to purchase release from the program. As in the early penitentiary and the Lancasterian school, constant staff monitoring and grading were the rule.

The market metaphors of the Lancasterian system pervaded the school building and relations in it. Students sat at lunchroom benches according to their rank, wore school-issue shirts of a color signifying their rank, engaged in mock auctions in which they traded points earned in the classroom and in assemblies for rewards of soda and candy, and monitored charts posted weekly with the names of those who had acquired the highest point scores and thereby earned a variety of prizes as well as credit toward early release from the program. Deals were transacted throughout the day: applause for a public speaker earned so many points; so many more could be earned by offering a handshake to an important school visitor. Demerits in the form of physical labor were exchanged for instances of school disobedience: a day of lawn-mowing was the price for being caught with a package of illicit cigarettes, an afternoon mopping floors could be exchanged for an argument on a school van.

School rules, about which students were continually being reminded by watchful staff, tended to be picayune and to focus on controlling physical activity. Many had to do with such minute matters as what clothing and jewelry students were allowed to wear, what forms of address they were to use with adults, and how they were to position their hats when sitting in a classroom or on a school van. Rewards and punishments were specific rather than diffuse: individual behaviors and acts of speech were scored at least hourly for the degree to which they exemplified compliance. Stressing individual achievement and performance to minute specifications, the marketplace in merit promised to serve in its contemporary setting, as it had in its original setting, as an alternative to the physical brutality, caprice, and disorder characteristic of many other formal institutions for the poor, the criminal, or the delinquent.

The daily behavioral system embodied empowerment as well as incapacitation. Students were free to participate in the marketplace of rewards and punishments with the assumption that they were rational actors, unencumbered by stereotypes prevailing in the social world outside the school about the moral deficiencies or untrustworthiness of delinquents; but they were at the same time tethered to picayune regulations over which they had had no input and about which they were allowed no comment.

Pedagogical interactions were organized similarly around the prevailing school theme of commodity exchange and the conjunction of empowerment and incapacitation. Concerned about matters of quality assurance, school district officials supervising the Academy contract had required that students be enrolled in courses officially matched to those on district rolls. Yet diverse student skill levels and high mobility rates—in part a reflection of the students' constantly evolving legal status—militated against the traditional classroom arrangement of instruction organized deliberately around a sequence of topics or skills scheduled over a calendar year. There was virtually no classroom instruction, and evaluation of student academic work was minimal or gratuitous; all academic course content was divided into minute fragments that could be completed in very short periods, often as little as several minutes, by students working alone at their seats and with no involvement by teachers. Critical or intellectual engagement was not required from students. Some of the required worksheets, having been used over and over, already had correct answers scribbled on them, making it unnecessary for students even to bother reading any of the worksheet text. Students completed their work on pieces of looseleaf paper that they submitted to teachers, if at all, at the end of each class period.

Academy students had a chance this way to earn formal course credits potentially transferable to regular public school. But a great many had little incentive to work toward school credit, since it was highly unlikely, either because they were too old or too far behind or because school administrators had locked them out, that they would ever make it back successfully into mainstream public school. Being forced to engage in unit completion and credit acquisition tended to reinforce for many students, in this context, the prevailing commodity form of trading alienated labor exclusively for the sake of external symbolic payments.

There was widespread resistance to the unit system and the marketplace rules of performance. Students remained generally unwilling to give themselves wholeheartedly to rules that were stultifying and chores that held little personal value or meaning. Like workers in the formal economy who perform boring, repetitive labor not for its intrinsic worth but for the payments it might bring later, students engaged at times in a variety of acts of workplace sabotage. They dragged their feet, pretended not to hear certain directives, faked their classwork, pushed behavioral rules to the limit, and poked fun at their teachers and themselves. They complied minimally, for the most part, with what was asked of them, sometimes exaggerating deference and obedience in displays of ironic mastery. Laughter and sarcasm at the institution's expense were tools of generally minor yet almost daily rebellion, in assemblies and in classrooms. Flagin' (camouflaging or faking) was an expression of student self-mastery in a context where there were, realistically, few other options that had no damaging legal ramifications.

Like managers in the formal economy who supervise sometimes recalcitrant workers, staff could be subjected to discipline from their own supervisors when student compliance lagged. Teachers occasionally attempted in response to clamp down on their slowest producers. Their efforts tended to be unsuccessful, however, since school managers enforced ethics and safety rules and insisted on humane treatment that did not involve physical or emotional coercion, the traditional strategies in juvenile justice and in some schools. Moreover, when students were defiant and sarcastic, and when minimal compliance was accompanied routinely by irony and exaggeration, it became difficult for teachers to claim with certainty that the school's educational and rehabilitative goals had been achieved, even when points and school credits, strictly speaking, had been acquired.

Reacting to the quandary that defined their encounters, teachers developed strategies by which to claim greater work autonomy, ease some of the daily difficulties of the job, and secure for their labors a more sure sense of meaning and accomplishment. They mitigated the rigidities of the prevailing market system by deviating from official rules, asserting the authority to administer rewards and punishments inconsistently, based on personal judgment instead of on official or standard prescriptions of point-and-rank exchange. Circumventing the discipline of their supervisors, they kept classroom mishaps a secret. Minimizing their connection to a juvenile justice system widely regarded as brutal and inconsistent, they distanced themselves, in their conversations, from troubling aspects of the job and the setting.

Seeking to invest their work with significance and moral meaning, teachers permeated the school program with religious imagery and rituals. Breaking with public school convention as well as laws mandating the separation of church and state, they introduced evangelical Christian themes and displays throughout the building: there were frequent prayers by students as well as staff, gospel music in the classrooms, field trips to religious events and speeches, and performances by visiting evangelists. Graduation ceremonies modeled after Baptist conversion rituals were a forum during which the most successful students could attest, alongside their teachers, that the program had led them to some important transformation perhaps more profound than what was being measured in the strictly economistic calculus of points and rank. Christian religious displays rendered school processes morally significant and worthy in terms meaningful to the staff, despite the vexing tendency of irony to accompany obedience in the classroom and in the absence of reliable traditional school outcome measures.

As they struggled under very difficult circumstances to derive a sense of accomplishment and significance from their daily labors, Academy teachers achieved a logical transformation: they connected practical ground-level building procedures to the more operationally elusive juvenile justice policy aim of changing children's lives. Religious displays may have constituted a legal violation, but they were not antithetical to goals espoused in the officially secular terminology of the public schools and the juvenile justice system. On the contrary, they had political and dramaturgical significance: if the juvenile justice system, with all its troubles, could not by itself guarantee a satisfying or substantive justice for young people, then at least the Academy staff could attest that changes of some kind had been achieved. If the public schools could not guarantee that students would come away from years of schooling with even minimal levels of literacy and numeracy, then Academy staff could attest at least that they had enabled some drama of personal growth that others had not apparently achieved.

Certain forms of cultural knowledge were embodied, it can be said, in the daily school curriculum as practiced. Students were reminded at every turn of their looseleaf sheets that they would have to learn to live with profound and almost mind-numbing drudgery. All who finished the program came away having practiced accommodating themselves, for a short period at least, to the disciplining rhythms of selling their labor in a marketplace where others would determine the sometimes bizarre or personally insulting rules of reward and exchange and where pleasure could be sought not in the work itself but in the temporal interstices of the work, in the momentary individualized snatching of relief. Institutions have an ideal character image that guides their members in selecting which features of behavior to reward and which to punish. The rule system at Academy empowered students with a level of much-needed responsibility and freedom to choose to some degree their behavior and accept its consequences. But it did not grant them authority to scrutinize, criticize, or actively amend the regulations of daily life that others had made for them. Too much criticism or complaining was itself an offense punishable through the point system. This was no civics lesson, then, in the kind of critical empowerment most Americans associate with responsible citizenship in a democracy. On the other hand, neither was it an experience of strict incapacitation. Rather, it was a practical lesson in the rather degraded self-discipline to which most of the children would likely have to accommodate in their transition to a young adulthood in the city.

Successful students came away from Academy having practiced taking on the technical-rational orientation to language and performance that characterizes formal marketplace transactions. With constant monitoring and point-card scoring, having continually to sell their performances of compliance, they had to exercise the kind of deliberate, calculated, and alert self-interest that is a hallmark of middle-class life and that makes up part of the cultural capital most middle-class children acquire at an early age. At the same time, however, as they rehearsed the behavioral characteristics of the middle class, there was no suggestion that they deserved or had a right to demand for themselves any of the authentic trappings of middle-class life—market access unencumbered by racial or gender bias, just and timely legal

hearings, and the expectation that school might offer rich
academic support and personally rewarding learning experiences leading to genuine skills increases and intellectual
growth. The Academy program participated in this sense in
sustaining the long-standing American educational illusion
that individual behavior and attitudes are the primary source
of success, rather than genuine opportunity, great schooling,
and racial and social equity.

By all accounts, Academy's children had had devastating
personal experiences of family strife, poverty, school failure,
and rejection, and in some cases sexual violence. The failures
of self-control that had landed them in the juvenile justice
system had been at least aggravated and perhaps enabled by
shortcomings in larger civic, educational, legal, and economic
institutions. But Academy transformed these complex, broad,
and multiple system failings into smaller-scale prescriptions
for individualized educational and rehabilitative services.
Problems of justice and equity became cast as a matter of each
student learning to do his or her schoolwork and behave. Even
as they held out to students the possibility of religious renewal
and insisted for the most part on treating students as rational
and worthy of affection, Academy teachers achieved, in a
sense, a political diversion: their work displaced policy attention onto the educationally neediest and psychologically most
degraded of children and shifted it away from more complicated, powerful, or politically contentious targets.

The earnestness of most of the staff and the New Testament
promise of dignity and redemption held open to children the
possibility, perhaps, of some personal psychological renewal
and reunification with the community. But kindness, forgiveness, and a commodity system of rewards for good behavior did not teach illiterates to read and write; nor did they

impart substantive vocational skills. In what was ostensibly one of the better facilities of its kind in the state–a school where interagency coordination was to some degree the norm, where staff idealism and cooperation were routine, where personnel had been designated to look after special-education students, and where hands-on managers enforced official ethics and safety rules–in the final analysis, the young people's federally guaranteed rights to an appropriate education were by no stretch of the imagination actually being met. This was particularly the case for students with special educational needs. Keeping Academy students on public school enrollment lists, a variety of state and local agencies were able in part to meet formal mandates about schooling them. Little evidence was found, however, that students were leaving Academy having mastered any authentic school subject content, that their completion of minute, mechanical assignments translated into an understanding of any academic concepts or higher-order principles, or that they had acquired skills that would enable them to seek and hold stable jobs guaranteeing a minimally livable wage. It remains to be seen whether juvenile justice and educational institutions in the future will be able to do better.

Notes

Chapter One

1. The names of people and locations have been replaced with pseudonyms to protect privacy. Information that could clearly distinguish Academy from other educational programs has been omitted.

2. Several in-depth studies of the culture in alternative schools have been conducted, most notably by Kelly (1993) and by Gold and Mann (1984), focusing on "last chance" schools, and by Everhart (1988), focusing on "schools of choice." For descriptions of the organization and structure of alternative school programs, see Young (1990) and Barr (1981). Critics warn about the political uses of alternative placements in reducing the appearance of high district dropout rates and note the possibility that some students are actively "pushed out" to the point of becoming dropouts. For discussions, see Fine (1991), Kelly (1993), Arnove and Strout (1980), and Duke and Muzio (1978). A large body of literature on school dropouts characterizes institutions as "safety valves" for mainstream schools or as "dumping grounds" for difficult students. For review, see Eckstrom, Goerta, Pollack, and Rock (1986).

3. Section 504 of the Rehabilitation Act of 1974 (29 USC 794) guaranteed that handicapped minors would have rights to special educational services under a range of circumstances. The Education for All Handicapped Children Act of 1975 (PL 94-142) extended the right to special educational services to incarcerated persons age twenty-one and younger, excluding those deemed "socially maladjusted." The "social maladjustment" exclusion in PL 94-142

has been the source of a great deal of confusion and institutional wrangling and has resulted, according to some researchers, in a kind of "classification plea bargaining" (Gartner and Lipsky 1987) and denial of access to educational services to a range of children in need (Nelson and Rutherford 1990). The federal Office of Correctional Education was established in 1980. The Education for All Handicapped Children Act was replaced in 1990 by the Individuals with Disabilities Act (IDEA); 1997 amendments to IDEA also affected delivery of educational services in juvenile justice settings. For discussions, see National Association of State Directors of Special Education (1998) and Robinson and Rapport (1999).

4. Educational services to troubled teens removed from mainstream classes take a wide variety of forms around the nation (e.g., full-day public alternative schools, alternative schools run by private contractors in juvenile justice treatment facilities, half-day vocational classes in correctional institutions); are housed in diverse facilities (e.g., detention centers, drug treatment centers, rehabilitation camps, day treatment facilities, training schools); are located at a variety of points within the educational and criminal justice systems (diversion, adjudication, disposition, re-entry); and are regulated or supervised by an array of local, state, and federal agencies, sometimes working together, representing juvenile justice, education, law enforcement, or social services. There are an estimated three to four thousand such public or private programs currently nationwide, with a great deal of diversity in their organizational structure and in the configuration of their governmental affiliations (for review, see Coffey and Gemignani 1994). For discussions and examples of the diversity in educational programming in such contexts, see Rider-Hankins (1992); Bullock, Arends, and Mills (1983); Rutherford, Nelson, and Wolford (1986); Nelson, Rutherford, and Wolford (1987).

5. Local events mirrored those taking place around the nation. Children's rights advocates in the 1970s and 1980s brought to public attention a host of abuses at training schools in many states, eventually forcing the scaling back of many reform schools and a revamping of the structure and ideology of the juvenile justice system. There was also at this point a major rethinking of the so-called "rehabilitative" mission of the original juvenile court, with criticisms focused around the intrusiveness of state power, the assumption of paternalistic medical models of individual moral or physical deficit, and

the tendency of physical and emotional abuse to be imposed in the name of "therapy" or "treatment" (Ferdinand 1991; Sutton 1988).

6. For a review of some problems in detention centers, see United States Department of Justice Office of Juvenile Justice and Delinquency Prevention (1994, 1995b).

7. Geographic differences in the treatment and handling of juvenile offenders and in the timing of their judicial processing have been documented on a national scale, as have apparent racial biases. For discussions, see Krisberg (1987); Sampson (1993); Fagan, Slaughter, and Hartstone (1987); Butts and Halemba (1994); Hawkins (1987); Bishop and Frazier (1988); and Frazier, Bishop, and Henretta (1992).

8. There is a large body of research and considerable ideological debate regarding the degree to which discretionary authority at various points in the juvenile justice system might (or in fact should) contribute to irregular system outcomes (for discussion, see Feld 1990, 1993; Zimring 1994).

9. Studies in a variety of contexts have demonstrated that programs designed to divert children away from the juvenile justice system have sometimes had the opposite effect of "widening the net" of state control (Blomberg 1983; Klein, Teilman, Styles, Bugas Lincoln, and Labin-Rosensweig 1973).

10. Estimates vary somewhat. For discussions, see Leone, Rutherford, and Nelson (1991); Bullock and McArthur (1994); and McIntyre (1993).

11. On the national scale, there is a pervasive and acute lack of understanding within the juvenile justice system of the educational needs of children with disabilities, and shortcomings in the design, implementation, and delivery of educational and treatment services to disabled students are widely documented (Rider-Hankins 1992; Platt, Wienke, and Tunick 1982).

12. I am a white Jewish middle-class woman from a Northern state; the students and staff were mostly Baptist and from the South. There were relatively few Jews in the community as a whole, and the issue of my religion did arise: one of the teachers told me his wife had once worked with a Jewish woman and "liked her." I tried to stay low-key, and I participated in the Christian religious ceremonies that were held daily in staff meetings and school assemblies; it did not take me long to learn to recite the prayers along with the rest of the group.

13. For a critique of the individual-psychology–centered approach to the study of student behavior in institutions, see Noguera (1995); Wehlage and Rutter (1987); and Wehlage, Rutter, Smith, Lesko, and Fernandez (1989). An alternate approach is to examine the mutually socially constructed nature of interactions and the political or organizational contexts in which people and behavior are officially defined as problematic. See McLaren (1986), Fine (1991), and Cicourel (1968), the latter being among the most widely cited analyses of this type in juvenile justice settings.

14. For consideration of the "ecology" of institutions, see Sarason (1971) and Bronfonbrenner (1979). For a practical application of this approach, see Lipsitz (1984). The literature on "effective schools" draws in part from this analytical model of the nested interactions of organizations, contexts, and personalities.

15. For a more general discussion of participant observation as a research methodology applied to educational contexts, see Spindler (1987), Bogdan and Biklen (1992), and Sherman and Webb (1990). Ferrell and Hamm (1998) note the difficulties of gaining effective research access in criminal justice settings and the benefits of participant observation in such settings.

Chapter Two

1. On the characteristics of children in the juvenile justice system, see United States Department of Justice Office of Juvenile Justice and Delinquency Prevention (1995a, 1995b). There are indications that black males may be overrepresented in treatment programs and facilities run by government agencies, whereas whites and females are reportedly more concentrated in programs and facilities run by private contractors (Leone, Rutherford, and Nelson 1991; Coffey and Gemignani 1994; National Association of State Directors of Special Education 1998).

2. Jacobs (1990) documents the ramifications of institutional wrangling over admissions criteria and definitions of need in juvenile justice settings, noting that the concept of institutional "good citizenship" can lead service providers to embrace certain children even as they reject others.

3. Studies on a national scale of juveniles having trouble staying in school indicate that the academic skills levels of such students range widely (see, e.g., Natriello 1987; Leone 1990).

4. For a discussion of "gifted" students in alternative education, see Osborne and Byrnes (1990).

5. Gartner and Lipsky (1987) discuss the prevalence of such problems on a national scale, noting that lack of attention to paper trails and minimal participation by families in the IEP process are part of the much larger failure of special education as it is currently designed, organized, and delivered in the United States. See also Robinson and Rapport (1999).

6. For one estimate of the prevalence of mental retardation in juvenile justice settings, see McIntyre (1993).

7. Numerous studies indicate that a large proportion of children in juvenile justice custody have been victims of abuse or neglect and, conversely, that children who are abused or neglected are far more likely than others to enter the criminal justice system once they become adults (United States Department of Justice Office of Juvenile Justice and Delinquency Prevention 1995a).

8. Miller (1998) documents the bitterness and sense of institutional hypocrisy that many children bring with them when they enter juvenile justice programs, and the degree to which this sensibility affects social interactions in such settings.

9. There is a large body of literature on the social reproduction of gender relations in schools and other institutional settings. For examples and discussion, see Holland and Eisenhart (1988), Kelly (1993), Weis (1988), and Wolpe (1988).

10. Recruitment of minorities into the teaching profession has become a well-known priority for educational organizations and institutions, but white staffs continue to dominate public schools on the national scale, including schools where students of color are the majority. Staffing problems have been well-known at alternative schools and in correctional education (for a discussion of training needs, see Roberts and Bullock 1987). One writer has discussed the issue of administrators assigning teachers to alternative schools as a way to punish them (Weber 1972).

Chapter Three

1. For a discussion of educational or treatment programs using token economies, see Mulvey, Arthur, and Repucci (1993); Rider-Hankins (1992); and United States Department of Justice Office of Juvenile Justice and Delinquency Prevention (1995b).

2. There is a rich historiographic and philosophical debate on the cultural underpinnings of the behavioral model of penology, with writers linking the development of indeterminate sentencing and surveillance-based discipline to an emerging modern industrial social order. For examples, see Dumm (1987), Foucault (1979), Duff and Garland (1994), Garland (1990), Katz (1968), Sutton (1988), Platt (1969), Morris and Rothman (1998), and Rothman (1980).

Chapter Four

1. The term "individualized instruction" is vague and overused in education in general, given to a wide array of school practices, many of them dull and routine, even in private schools for the middle class (for comparison, see Everhart 1988). Several Academy staff members, including Kevin, the education director, as well as administrators in the school's parent firm, with whom I was in contact, were aware that the unit system was stultifying and old-fashioned, and they talked of their hope someday to be able to replace the existing units with a more activity-rich curriculum that would still meet with school district and state-agency approval. Despite these stated intentions, there was no deviation from the unit system during this study.

2. This phenomenon has been widely described in the literature in education, particularly in studies of classroom management, and has been called, alternately, the "bargain to learn," the "uneasy truce," the "negotiated order of the classroom," "agreement," and "the conspiracy of convenience" (for a variety of characterizations, see Cusick 1973; Dreeben 1968, 1973; Denscombe 1985; Jackson 1990; Sizer 1992; Sarason 1971; Everhart 1983a, 1987; Foley 1990; McNeil 1981; Sedlak, Wheeler, Pullin, and Cusick 1985; Waller 1965).

Chapter Five

1. The concept of "ritual supplies" and the construction of oppositional or distinctive personal identities in carceral settings have been studied in some depth over the last half century since the publication of Sykes's (1958) landmark study of inmates and guards in a maximum security prison.

2. In his analysis of the behavior of mental patients, Goffman (1961) attaches the label "secondary adjustments" to the unauthorized means that a member of an organization uses in order to get "around the organization's assumptions as to what he should do and get and hence what he should be" (p. 189).

3. Several contemporary writers have embedded their analyses of such quasi-oppositional activity in a broader political-economic framework, calling attention to class-based patterns of resistance and accommodation to the organization of political or social power (Scott 1985), the organization of the workplace (Paules 1991), and the organization of gender identity (Smith-Rosenberg 1975). Others have described such activity more broadly in the context of identity and class formation (Scott 1988; Thompson 1966; Wexler 1987). Educational writers have documented the ways in which apparently rebellious actions by students in school settings can have the effect of reproducing class relationships (e.g., Willis 1977), gender relationships (e.g., Holland and Eisenhart 1988), and race relationships (e.g., Ogbu 1974; Weis 1985). Among studies of classroom climate that have been conducted from within this framework, Everhart's (1983a, 1983b, 1987) analyses of "goofing off" behavior by early adolescents in the white working class most explicitly links student disruption to the concept of "reified knowledge," arguing that student reactions to dull work routines reproduce the broader cultural separation of use value from exchange value and reflect the alienated labor process in a capitalist social regime.

Chapter Six

1. For further discussion of the logical problem of translating ground-level institutional practices to theory-level public policy mandates, see Goffman (1961) and Jacobs (1990). For a philosophical characterization of the problem, see Garland (1990).

2. Many writers focusing on teaching as a form of employment (e.g., Apple 1979, 1982) have noted the tendency of teachers to engage in sometimes ironic responses to the proletarianization of their work.

3. For a description of a similar dilemma among prison guards, see Sykes (1958).

4. When they use knowledge of a student's troubled past or home life to temper their reactions to disobedience, teachers are in

fact negotiating two logical tensions at the heart of punishment and criminal justice—first, the tension between free will and societal determinants of action; and second, the tension between consistency and case-specific appropriateness in choosing a response. Acknowledging the negative effects of poverty or family strife means, necessarily, absolving the offender from some measure of blame for his or her crime; but if the offender is not wholly to blame, then individual punishment is essentially misplaced or, worse, pointless. On the other hand, acknowledging only individual blame means, necessarily, denying the sometimes obvious environmental or societal influences on an offender's actions. Moreover, meting out consistent punishments for crime means, in many cases, ignoring the distinctive circumstances under which crimes are committed. But meting out punishments tailored ostensibly to each case can mean, ultimately, being capricious and unfair. For further discussions, see Matza (1964), Reiman (1995), and Garland (1990).

5. Compare Jacobs's (1990) analysis of redemption narratives among probation workers.

6. Leone (1990) notes the negative effects on child welfare that result from the prevailing fragmentation of professional expertise and authority.

Chapter Seven

1. Problems associated with the identification and definition of outcome measures have been documented widely in the literature on delinquency treatment and prevention (for review, see Mulvey, Arthur, and Repucci 1993).

2. Studies on the national scale indicate that many children in juvenile justice never finish traditional high schools or earn degrees according to the usual timetable, although some continue their education in other venues, such as by taking the GED exam (Leone, Rutherford, and Nelson 1991).

References

Altschuler, D., and Armstrong, T. 1984. "Intervening with Serious Juvenile Offenders." In *Violent Juvenile Offenders*, ed. R. Mathias, P. Demuro, and R. Allinson, 61–70. San Francisco: National Council on Crime and Delinquency.

Apple, M. 1979. *Ideology and Curriculum*. Boston: Routledge and Kegan Paul.

Apple, M. 1982. *Education and Power*. Boston: Routledge and Kegan Paul.

Apple, M., and Weis, L. 1983. *Ideology and Practice in Schooling*. Philadelphia: Temple University Press.

Arnove, R., and Strout, T. 1980. "Alternative Schools for Disruptive Youth." *Educational Forum* 44: 452–71.

Bakal, Y., and Lowell, H. 1992. "The Private Sector in Juvenile Corrections." In *Juvenile Justice and Public Policy: Toward a National Agenda*, ed. I. M. Schwartz, 196–213. New York: Lexington Books, Maxwell Macmillan International.

Barr, R. 1981. "Alternatives for the Eighties: A Second Decade of Development." *Phi Delta Kappan* 62(8): 57–73.

Bernard, T. J. 1992. *The Cycle of Juvenile Justice*. New York: Oxford University Press.

Bishop, D., and Frazier, C. 1988. "The Influence of Race in Juvenile Justice Processing." *Journal of Research in Crime and Delinquency* 25: 242–63.

Blomberg, T. G. 1983. "Diversion's Disparate Results and Unresolved Questions: An Integrative Evaluation Perspective." *Journal of Research in Crime and Delinquency* 20(1): 24–38.

Bogdan, R., and Biklen, S. K. 1992. *Qualitative Research for Education*. Boston: Allyn and Bacon.

Bourdieu, P., and Passeron, J. 1977. *Reproduction in Education, Society and Culture*. Beverly Hills: Sage Publications.

Bowles, S., and Gintis, H. 1976. *Schooling in Capitalist America*. New York: Basic Books.

Bronfenbrenner, U. 1979. *The Ecology of Human Development*. Cambridge: Harvard University Press.

Bullock, T., Arends, R., and Mills, F. 1983. "Implementing Educational Services in a Detention Facility." *Juvenile Justice and Family Court Journal* 8: 21–29.

Bullock, L., and McArthur, P. 1994. "Correctional Special Education: Disability Prevalence Estimates and Teachers' Preparation Programs." *Education and Treatment of Children* 17: 347–55.

Butts, J., and Halemba, G. 1994. "Delays in Juvenile Justice: Findings from a National Survey." *Juvenile and Family Court Journal* 45: 31–46.

Carnoy, M., and Levin, H. 1985. *Schooling and Work in the Democratic State*. Stanford, Calif.: Stanford University Press.

Cicourel, A. 1968. *The Social Organization of Juvenile Justice*. New York: Wiley.

Coffey, O., and Gemignani, M. 1994. *Effective Practices in Juvenile Correctional Education: A Study of the Literature and Research 1980–1992*. Washington, D.C.: United States Department of Justice Office of Juvenile Justice and Delinquency Prevention.

Coulby, D., and Harper, T. 1985. *Preventing Classroom Disruption: Policy Practice and Evaluation in Urban Schools*. London: Croom Helm.

Cusick, P. 1973. *Inside High School: The Student's World*. New York: Holt, Rinehart and Winston.

de Beaumont, G., and de Tocqueville, A. 1964. *On the Penitentiary System in the United States and Its Application in France*. Carbondale: Southern Illinois University Press, 59–60.

Denscombe, M. 1985. *Classroom Control: A Sociological Perspective*. London: Allen and Unwin.

Dreeben, R. 1968. *On What Is Learned in School*. Reading, Mass.: Addison Wesley.

Dreeben, R. 1973. "The School as a Workplace." In *Second Handbook of Research on Teaching: A Project of the American Educational Research Association,* ed. R. Travers, 450–73. Chicago: Rand McNally.

Duff, R. A., and Garland, D., eds. 1994. *A Reader on Punishment.* London: Oxford University Press.

Duke, D., and Muzio, I. 1978. "How Effective Are Alternative Schools: A Review of Recent Evaluations and Reports." *Teachers College Record* 79(3): 461–83.

Dumm, T. L. 1987. *Democracy and Punishment: Disciplinary Origins of the United States.* Madison: University of Wisconsin Press.

Durkheim, E. 1984. *The Division of Labor in Society.* New York: Free Press.

Eckstrom, R., Goerta, M., Pollack, J., and Rock, D. 1986. "Who Drops Out of High School and Why? Findings from a National Study." *Teachers College Record* 87(3): 356–73.

Erikson, K. 1968. *Wayward Puritans.* New York: Wiley.

Everhart, R. 1983a. *Reading, Writing and Resistance.* Boston: Routledge and Kegan Paul.

Everhart, R. 1983b. "Classroom Management, Student Opposition, and the Labor Process." In *Ideology and Practice in Schooling,* ed. M. Apple and L. Weis, 169–92. Philadelphia: Temple University Press.

Everhart, R. 1987. "Understanding Student Disruption and Classroom Control." *Harvard Educational Review* 57(1): 77–83.

Everhart, R. 1988. *Practical Ideology and Symbolic Community: An Ethnography of Schools of Choice.* New York: Falmer Press.

Fagan, J., Slaughter E., and Hartstone, E. 1987. "Blind Justice: The Impact of Race on the Juvenile Process." *Crime and Delinquency* 33: 224–58.

Feld, B. 1990. "The Punitive Juvenile Court and the Quality of Procedural Justice: Disjunction Between Rhetoric and Reality." *Crime and Delinquency* 36(4): 443–66.

Feld, B. 1993. "Juvenile (In)Justice and the Criminal Court Alternative." *Crime and Delinquency* 39(4): 403–24.

Ferdinand, T. N. 1991. "History Overtakes the Juvenile Justice System." *Crime and Delinquency* 37(2): 204–24.

Ferrell, J., and Hamm, M. 1998. *Ethnography at the Edge: Crime, Deviance, and Filed Research.* Boston: Northeastern University Press.

Fine, M. 1991. *Framing Dropouts: Notes on the Politics of an Urban High School.* Albany: State University of New York Press.

Flake, C. 1984. *Redemptorama.* New York: Penguin Books.

Foley, D. 1990. *Learning Capitalist Culture: Deep in the Heart of Tejas.* Philadelphia: University of Pennsylvania Press.

Foucault, M. 1979. *Discipline and Punish.* New York: Vintage Books.

Frazier, C., Bishop, D., and Henretta, J. 1992. "The Social Context of Race Differentials in Juvenile Justice Dispositions." *Sociological Quarterly* 33(3): 447–58.

Garland, D. 1990. *Punishment and Modern Society: A Study in Social Theory.* New York: Oxford University Press.

Gartner, A., and Lipsky, D. 1987. "Beyond Special Education: Toward a Quality System for All Students." *Harvard Educational Review* 57(4): 367–95.

Gemignani, R. 1994. *Juvenile Correctional Education: A Time for Change.* Washington, D.C.: United States Department of Justice Office of Juvenile Justice and Delinquency Prevention.

Goffman, E. 1961. *Asylums.* Garden City: Anchor.

Gold, M., and Mann, D. 1984. *Expelled to a Friendlier Place: A Study of Effective Alternative Schools.* Ann Arbor: University of Michigan Press.

Grantham, D. 1994. *The South in Modern America: A Region at Odds.* New York: HarperPerennial.

Greenwood, P. 1988. *Correctional Programs for Chronic Juvenile Offenders: Characteristics of Three Exemplary Programs.* Santa Monica, Calif.: Rand Corporation.

Greenwood, P., and Zimring, F. 1985. *One More Chance: The Pursuit of Promising Intervention Strategies for Chronic Juvenile Offenders.* Santa Monica, Calif.: Rand Corporation.

Habermas, J. 1984. *The Theory of Communicative Action,* vol. 1. Boston: Beacon Press.

Habermas, J. 1987. *The Theory of Communicative Action,* vol. 2. Boston: Beacon Press.

Hall, R., and Stack, C. 1982. *Holding on to the Land and the Lord: Kinship, Ritual, Land Tenure, and Social Policy in the Rural South.* Athens: University of Georgia Press.

Hawkins, D. 1987. "Beyond Anomalies: Rethinking the Conflict Perspective on Race and Criminal Punishment." *Social Forces* 65: 719–45.

Hellriegel, K., and Yates, J. 1999. "Collaboration Between Correctional and Public School Systems Serving Juvenile Offenders: A Case Study." *Education and Treatment of Children* 22(1): 55–83.

Hill, D. 1998. "Reform Schools." *Teacher Magazine* 9(8): 34–41.

Hogan, D. 1989. "The Market Revolution and Disciplinary Power: Joseph Lancaster and the Psychology of the Early Classroom System." *History of Education Quarterly* 29(3): 381–417.

Holland, D., and Eisenhart, M. 1988. "Women's Way of Going to School: Cultural Reproduction of Women's Identities as Workers." In *Class, Race, and Gender in American Education*, ed. L. Weis, 266–301. Albany: State University of New York Press.

Hunter, J. 1983. *American Evangelism: Conservative Religion and the Quandary of Modernity.* New Brunswick, N.J.: Rutgers University Press.

Ingersoll, S., and LeBoeuf, D. 1997. *Reaching Out to Youth Out of the Educational Mainstream.* Washington, D.C.: United States Department of Justice Office of Juvenile Justice and Delinquency Prevention.

Jackson, P. 1990. *Life in Classrooms.* New York: Teachers College Press.

Jacobs, M. 1990. *Screwing the System and Making It Work: Juvenile Justice in the No-Fault Society.* Chicago: University of Chicago Press.

Kaestle, C. 1983. *Pillars of the Republic: Common Schools and American Society.* New York: Hill and Wang.

Katz, M. 1968. *The Irony of Early School Reform: Educational Innovation in Mid–19th Century Massachusetts.* Cambridge: Harvard University Press.

Kelly, D. 1993. *Last Chance High: How Girls and Boys Drop In and Out of Alternative Schools.* New Haven, Conn.: Yale University Press.

Klein, M., Teilman, K., Styles, J., Bugas Lincoln, S., and Labin-Rosensweig, S. 1973. "The Explosion in Police Diversion Programs: Evaluating the Structural Dimensions of a Social Fad." In *The Juvenile Justice System,* ed. M. Klein, 101–20. Beverly Hills: Sage Publications.

Kosmin, B., and Lachman, S. 1993. *One Nation Under God: Religion in Contemporary America.* New York: Harmony Books.

Krisberg, B. 1987. "The Incarceration of Minority Youth." *Crime and Delinquency* 33: 173–205.

Lawrence, J., Steed, D., and Young, P. 1984. *Disruptive Children, Disruptive Schools.* London: Croom Helm.

Leone, P. 1990. *Understanding Troubled and Troubling Youth.* Newbury Park, Calif.: Sage Publications.

Leone, P., Price, T., and Vitolo, R. 1986. "Appropriate Education of All Incarcerated Youth: Meeting the Spirit of P.L. 94-142 in Youth Detention Facilities." *Remedial and Special Education* 7(4): 9–14.

Leone, P., Rutherford, R., and Nelson, C. 1991. *Special Education in Juvenile Corrections.* Reston, Va.: Council for Exceptional Children.

Lerman, P. 1984. "Child Welfare, the Private Sector and Community-based Corrections." *Crime and Delinquency* 30: 5–38.

Lipsitz, J. 1984. *Successful Schools for Young Adolescents*. New Brunswick, N.J.: Transaction Books.

Matza, D. 1964. *Delinquency and Drift*. New York: Wiley.

McIntyre, T. 1993. "Behaviorally Disordered Youth in Correctional Settings: Prevalence, Programming, and Teacher Training." *Behavioral Disorders* 18: 167–76.

McLaren, P. 1986. *Schooling as a Ritual Performance*. London: Routledge and Kegan Paul.

McNeil, L. 1981. "Negotiating Classroom Knowledge: Beyond Achievement and Socialization." *Journal of Curriculum Studies* 13: 313–28.

Miller, J. G. 1998. *Last One Over the Wall: The Massachusetts Experiment in Closing Reform Schools*. Columbus: Ohio State University Press.

Morris, N., and Rothman, D. 1998. *The Oxford History of the Prison: The Practice of Punishment in Western Society*. New York: Oxford University Press.

Mulvey, E. P., Arthur, M. W., and Repucci, N. D. 1993. "The Prevention and Treatment of Juvenile Delinquency: A Review of the Research." *Clinical Psychology Review* 13: 133–67.

National Association of State Directors of Special Education. 1998. "Students with Disabilities in Juvenile Justice Programs: Directions for Federal Support." Proceedings from the Policy Forum, October 26–27, Alexandria, Va. ERIC Documents.

National Conference of State Legislatures. 1999a. *Alternative Schools for Disruptive Students, Information Clearinghouse*. Denver, Colo.: Author.

National Conference of State Legislatures. 1999b. *Educational Services for Delinquent Youth, State Enactments*. Denver, Colo.: Author.

Natriello, G. 1987. *School Dropouts: Patterns and Policies*. New York: Teachers College Press.

Nelson, C. M., and Rutherford, R. B., Jr. 1990. "Troubled Youth in Public Schools: Emotionally Disturbed or Socially Maladjusted?" In *Understanding Troubled and Troubling Youth*, ed. P. Leone, 38–60. Newbury Park, Calif.: Sage Publications.

Nelson, C., Rutherford, R., and Wolford, B. 1987. *Special Education in the Criminal Justice System*. Columbus, Ohio: Merrill.

Noguera, P. 1995. "Preventing and Producing Violence: A Critical Analysis of Responses to School Violence." *Harvard Educational Review* 65(2): 189–212.

Ogbu, J. 1974. *The Next Generation: An Ethnography of Education in an Urban Neighborhood.* New York: Academic Press.

Ogbu, J. 1981. "School Ethnography: A Multilevel Approach." *Anthropology and Education Quarterly* 12(1): 3–29.

Osborne, J., and Byrnes, D. 1990. "Gifted, Disaffected, Disruptive Youths and the Alternative High School." *Gifted Child Today* 13(3): 45–48.

Paules, G. F. 1991. *Dishing It Out: Power and Resistance Among Waitresses in a New Jersey Restaurant.* Philadelphia: Temple University Press.

Platt, A. 1969. *The Child Savers: The Invention of Delinquency.* Chicago: University of Chicago Press.

Platt, J., Wienke, W., and Tunick, R. 1982. "Need for Training in Special Education for Correctional Educators." *Journal of Correctional Education* 32(4): 8–12.

Reiman, J. 1995. *The Rich Get Richer and the Poor Get Prison: Ideology, Crime and Criminal Justice.* Boston: Allyn and Bacon.

Rider-Hankins, P. 1992. *The Educational Process in Juvenile Correctional Schools.* Washington, D.C.: United States Department of Justice Office of Juvenile Justice and Delinquency Prevention.

Roberts, R., and Bullock, L. 1987. *Critical Skills of Corrections Education Personnel: A Survey of Perceived Needs.* Final Research Report. Rockville, Md.: National Institute of Justice.

Robinson, T., and Rapport, M. 1999. "Providing Special Education in the Juvenile Justice System." *Remedial and Special Education* 20(1): 19–26, 35.

Rothman, D. 1980. *Conscience and Convenience.* Boston: Little Brown.

Rotman, E. 1994. "Beyond Punishment." In *A Reader on Punishment,* ed. R. A. Duff and D. Garland, 284–305. New York: Oxford University Press.

Rutherford, R., Nelson, M., and Wolford, B. 1986. "Special Education in the Most Restrictive Environment." *Journal of Special Education* 19: 59–71.

Sampson, R. 1993. "Structural Variations in Juvenile Court Processing: Inequality, the Underclass and Social Control." *Law and Society Review* 27(2): 285–311.

Sarason, S. 1971. *The Culture of the School and the Problem of Change.* Boston: Allyn and Bacon.

Scott, J. C. 1985. *Weapons of the Weak: Everyday Forms of Peasant Resistance.* New Haven: Yale University Press.

Scott, J. W. 1988. *Gender and the Politics of History.* New York: Columbia University Press.

Sedlak, M., Wheeler, C., Pullin, D., and Cusick, P. 1985. "High School Reform and the 'Bargain to Learn.'" *Education and Urban Society* 17(2): 204–14.

Sherman, R., and Webb, R. 1990. *Qualitative Research in Education: Focus and Methods.* New York: Falmer Press.

Shoemaker, D. 1996. *Theories of Delinquency: An Examination of Explanations of Delinquent Behavior.* New York: Oxford University Press.

Sizer, T. R. 1992. *Horace's Compromise: The Dilemma of the American High School.* New York: Houghton Mifflin.

Smith, J. 1990. *The Frugal Gourmet on Our Immigrant Ancestors.* New York: William Morrow.

Smith-Rosenberg, C. 1975. *Disorderly Conduct: Visions of Gender in Victorian America.* New York: Oxford University Press.

Spindler, G. 1987. *Education and Cultural Process: Anthropological Approaches.* Prospect Heights, Ill.: Waveland Press.

Spring, J. 1990. *The American School, 1642–1990.* New York: Longman.

Sutton, J. 1988. *Stubborn Children: Controlling Delinquency in the United States, 1640–1981.* Berkeley: University of California Press.

Sykes, G. 1958. *The Society of Captives: A Study of a Maximum Security Prison.* Princeton: Princeton University Press.

Tapper, D., Kleinman, P., and Nakashian, M. 1997. "An Interagency Collaboration Strategy for Linking Schools with Social and Criminal Justice Services." *Social Work in Education* 19(3): 176–88.

Thompson, E. P. 1966. *The Making of the English Working Class.* New York: Vintage.

United States Department of Justice. 1988. *Report to the Nation on Crime and Justice: The Data.* Washington, D.C.: U.S. Government Printing Office.

United States Department of Justice. Office of Juvenile Justice and Delinquency Prevention. 1994. *Conditions of Confinement: Juvenile Detention and Corrections Facilities.* Washington, D.C.: U.S. Government Printing Office.

United States Department of Justice Office of Juvenile Justice and Delinquency Prevention. 1995a. *Juvenile Offenders and Victims: A National Report.* Washington, D.C.: U.S. Government Printing Office.

United States Department of Justice Office of Juvenile Justice and Delinquency Prevention. 1995b. *Guide for Implementing the Comprehensive Strategy for Serious, Violent and Chronic Juvenile Offenders.* Washington, D.C.: U.S. Government Printing Office.

Waller, W. 1965. *The Sociology of Teaching.* New York: Wiley.

Warboys, L., and Schauffer, C. 1986. "Legal Issues in Providing Special Education Services to Handicapped Inmates." *Remedial and Special Education* 7(3): 34–40.

Weber, E. 1972. "Dropouts Who Go to School." *Phi Delta Kappan* 53(9): 572–73.

Weber, M. 1976. *The Protestant Ethic and the Spirit of Capitalism.* New York: Charles Scribner's Sons.

Wehlage, G., and Rutter, R. A. 1987. "Dropping Out: How Much Do Schools Contribute to the Problem?" In *School Dropouts: Patterns and Policies,* ed. G. Natriello, 70–88. New York: Teachers College Press.

Wehlage, G., Rutter, R., Smith, G., Lesko, N., and Fernandez, R. 1989. *Reducing the Risk: Schools as Communities.* London: Falmer Press.

Weis, L. 1985. *Between Two Worlds: Black Students in an Urban Community College.* Boston: Routledge and Kegan Paul.

Weis, L. 1988. *Class, Race and Gender in American Education.* Albany: State University of New York Press.

Wexler, P. 1987. *Social Analysis of Education.* New York: Routledge.

Williams, C. 1982. "The Conversion Ritual in a Rural Black Baptist Church." In *Holding on to the Land and the Lord: Kinship, Ritual, Land Tenure, and Social Policy in the Rural South,* ed. R. Hall and C. Stack, 69–79. Athens: University of Georgia Press.

Willis, P. 1977. *Learning to Labor.* New York: Columbia University Press.

Wilson, C. R. 1995. *Judgment and Grace in Dixie: Southern Faiths from Faulkner to Elvis.* Athens: University of Georgia Press.

Wolpe, A. 1988. *Within School Walls: The Role of Discipline, Sexuality and the Curriculum.* London: Routledge and Kegan Paul.

Young, T. W. 1990. *Public Alternative Education: Options and Choice for Today's Schools.* New York: Teachers College Press.

Zimring, F. 1994. "Making the Punishment Fit the Crime: A Consumer's Guide to Sentencing Reform." In *A Reader on Punishment,* ed. R. A. Duff and D. Garland, 161–73. New York: Oxford University Press.

Index

abuse. *See* students, medical conditions of

academic achievement, 10, 29; measurement of, 155–56, 178n. *See also* English; math; oceanography; physical education; vocational education

admissions criteria, suspension of, 28–29, 178n

adolescence, 5–6

alternative education, 2, 3, 11, 19–20; antecedents to, 10; special diploma in, 30; studies of, 175–76n; trends in growth of, 3

alternative high school, 19, 20, 29, 77, 158–59. *See also* discipline

American Federation of Teachers, 3

American history: description of classroom instruction in, 81–82, 84–85, 112–13; description of curriculum in, 73–74

apathy, toward assignments, 76

assemblies, school: description of, 55–59; irony during, 58, 100, 10–103, 168

attendance statistics, 153–55

auctions, prize, 50

behavioral model of penology, 62–68, 180n

behavioral rules: flouting of, 93, 97, 126, 166, 168; list of, 49–50

boot camp, 15–16, 25, 68, 83–84, 121–22, 150

breakfast, 54–55

brokering, as classroom management strategy, 77

caseworker. *See* juvenile justice caseworker

Christian Coalition, 132

civil rights 4, 14, 135; movement, 8. *See also* lawsuits

classrooms, 2, 22; description of climate and teacher management of, 77–89, 121, 180n; physical description of, 42–45; primary task in, 77; shortages of in juvenile justice programs, 18

community service, 155

community-based programs, 4–5, 14

computers, donated, 45

continuing education, 158

contract, signing of, 47–48; as central metaphor in market system of school, 62–68